Financial Education in Europe

TRENDS AND RECENT DEVELOPMENTS

This work is published under the responsibility of the Secretary-General of the OECD. The opinions expressed and arguments employed herein do not necessarily reflect the official views of OECD member countries.

This document and any map included herein are without prejudice to the status of or sovereignty over any territory, to the delimitation of international frontiers and boundaries and to the name of any territory, city or area.

Please cite this publication as:
OECD (2016), *Financial Education in Europe: Trends and Recent Developments*, OECD Publishing, Paris.
http://dx.doi.org/10.1787/9789264254855-en

ISBN 978-92-64-25424-4 (print)
ISBN 978-92-64-25485-5 (PDF)

Photo credits: Cover © John Foxx/Stockbyte/Thinkstock

Corrigenda to OECD publications may be found on line at: *www.oecd.org/about/publishing/corrigenda.htm*.

Foreword

Constant evolution in the financial, economic, demographic and policy landscape, as well as gradual risk transfers to individuals, has turned financial literacy into a key life skill in today's societies. New and often complex financial products are being developed by financial service providers and new market players. This gives consumers, investors and small businesses greater access to a variety of payment solutions, credit offers and long-term savings and investment instruments. At the same time, individuals have to bear responsibility for a widening range of risks stemming from an uncertain economic and financial environment and shrinking welfare systems. These risks encompass job losses, unpredictable returns on investment, increasing life expectancy and related health risks. The impact of increasing life expectancy on an individual's responsibility to save for retirement is compounded in many countries by pension reforms resulting in a shift from Pay-As-You-Go to funded systems and from Defined Benefit to Defined Contribution systems.

This changing and challenging landscape requires that individuals and small businesses be equipped with the know-how, competence and motivation to make key financial decisions to help secure their financial future. Financial education policies that empower individuals and small businesses, coupled with enabling financial consumer protection frameworks, can effectively contribute to the financial well-being that supports financial stability and inclusive growth.

These developments are particularly pertinent to Europe, given the sophistication of retail financial markets, the impact of ageing populations, the reforms of public pension systems, and the pervading effect of the financial and economic crisis on household debt. Preliminary results from a 2015 OECD/INFE survey on adult financial literacy and inclusion show that European citizens often lack the financial awareness and skills to face these changes. In step with global trends and using the OECD/INFE Principles, 21 of the 48 European economies covered in this report are taking action by developing national strategies for financial education. Challenges remain, however, with respect to their implementation and effectiveness.

This report assesses trends in Europe which require financial education strategies and initiatives. It provides support to European policy makers looking to identify and design effective policies to improve financial literacy as a complement to financial consumer protection and inclusion.

This publication was delivered in April 2016 on the occasion of the "Netherlands-OECD Global Symposium on Financial Resilience throughout Life", taking place in Amsterdam and co-organised with the Money Wise Platform, part of the Ministry of Finance. This high-level global event, opened by H.M. Queen Maxima of the Netherlands and the OECD Secretary-General Angel Gurría during the Netherlands EU Presidency, is a testimony to the relevance of financial education policies in Europe, and of the role that they can play in ensuring better lives for its citizens.

Acknowledgements

This report was prepared under the direction of Ms. Flore-Anne Messy, Deputy Head of the Financial Affairs Division and Executive Secretary of the OECD International Network on Financial Education, and by Ms. Chiara Monticone, Policy Analyst. Mr. Andrea Grifoni, Policy Analyst, contributed to its finalisation. Mr. Edward Smiley provided technical support. The preparation of the report received financial support from VISA Europe Turkey and its member banks[1].

The report was developed thanks to the contributions of European members of the OECD International Network on Financial Education (OECD/INFE[2]).

The preliminary cross-comparable analysis of financial literacy and inclusion levels in the framework of the 2015 OECD/INFE Measurement exercise of the was made possible thanks to participating OECD/INFE members from Europe; these are: Bank of Albania; National Bank of Austria; Financial Services and Markets Authority of Belgium; Croatian National Bank and Croatian Financial Services Supervisory Agency; the Ministry of Finance of the Czech Republic; Ministry of Finance of Estonia; the Bank of France; the Hungarian National Bank; Financial and Capital Market Commission of the Republic of Latvia; Bank of Lithuania; Ministry of Finance of the Netherlands; AksjeNorge Norway; National Bank of Poland; Banco de Portugal, Portuguese Securities Market Commission and the Portuguese Insurance and Pension Funds Supervisory Authority; Capital Markets Board of Turkey; the Money Advice Service United Kingdom.

1. Members are Akbank T.A.Ş., Albaraka Türk Katılım Bankası A.Ş., Alternatifbank A.Ş., Anadolubank A.Ş., Asya Katılım Bankası A.Ş., Burgan Bank A.Ş., Citibank A.Ş., Denizbank A.Ş., Finansbank A.Ş., HSBC Bank A.Ş., ICBC Turkey Bank A.Ş., ING Bank AŞ., Kuveyt Türk Katılım Bankası A.Ş., Odea Bank A.Ş., Şekerbank T.A.Ş., T.C. Ziraat Bankası, Türk Ekonomi Bankası A.Ş., Türkiye Finans Katılım Bankası A.Ş., Türkiye Garanti Bankası A.Ş., Türkiye Halk Bankası A.Ş., Türkiye İş Bankası A.Ş., T. Vakıflar Bankası TAO, Yapı ve Kredi Bankası A.Ş.

2. The OECD International Network for financial education (OECD/INFE) was created in 2008 and as of January 2015 grouped together over 250 public institutions from 113 countries and economies. Member institutions meet regularly to share information and good practice and ultimately to develop policy evidence, analysis, research, and instruments on financial education.

Table of contents

Executive summary 7

Chapter 1. **Context and rationale for financial education in Europe** 9

1.1. Population ageing and pensions reforms 10
1.2. Household debt 11
1.3. Growing complexity of financial marketplace 12
1.4. Financial exclusion 13
1.5. Low financial literacy 15

Chapter 2. **Policy responses to financial education needs in Europe** 21

2.1. European Union policy responses on financial consumer protection, financial inclusion and financial education 22
2.2. National strategies for financial education 24
2.3. Financial education programmes 34

Chapter 3. **Policy and practical directions for financial education in Europe** 47

Policy and practical directions 48

Notes 51

References 52

Annex A. **Definition of Europe and OECD/INFE membership in Europe** 59

Annex B. **Sources of information by country** 60

Annex C. **Household debt data** 61

Annex D. **Financial inclusion data** 62

Annex E. **Financial knowledge questions in the 2015 OECD/INFE Toolkit for Measuring Financial Literacy and Financial Inclusion** 66

Tables

1.1. Financial knowledge level in European countries participating to the OECD/INFE 2015 Measurement Exercise 17
1.2. Financial behaviours in European countries participating to the OECD/INFE 2015 Measurement Exercise 18
2.1. National Strategies for financial education in Europe 24
2.2. Financial literacy assessments 30
2.3. Selected financial education websites and online tools 36
A.1. OECD/INFE membership in Europe 59
B.1. Sources of information by country 60

C.1. Household debt 61
D.1. Bank account holding, 2011 63
D.2. Bank account holding, 2005-2011 64
D.3. Financial products holding, 2011 65
E.1. Text of the financial knowledge questions 66

Figures

1.1. Household debt in selected European countries, 2004-2012 11
1.2. Bank account holding in selected European countries, in 2011 and 2014 14
1.3. Financial literacy proficiency levels among European 15-year-old students 16

Boxes

1.1. Financial knowledge and consumer debt in the United Kingdom 12
1.2. Demand-side barriers to financial inclusion in Russia 14
1.3. Financial literacy among 15-year-old students in Europe 16
2.1. Monitoring not-for-profit and private stakeholders 28
2.2. Synergies between financial consumer protection and financial education policies 32
2.3. Kenyan soap opera as financial education teaching resource in the United Kingdom 42
2.4. Impact evaluation of financial education in school in Europe 43

Executive summary

Given the growing interest in financial education in Europe and the rapid development of numerous initiatives by a diverse range of stakeholders, this report provides an overview of the most relevant and innovative policies and initiatives in the area of financial education and at the intersection between financial education, financial consumer protection and financial inclusion. Based on a wealth of experience, the report also offers some suggestions and highlights good practices for all stakeholders. This report complements other reports with a regional focus: Africa (Messy and Monticone, 2012), Latin America and the Caribbean (Garcia et al., 2013); and Asia and Pacific (Messy and Monticone, 2016).

Growing interest in financial literacy is reflected in the large European membership within the OECD International Network for Financial Education (OECD/INFE). Of the more than 110 OECD/INFE member economies, 40 come from Europe. Of these, most have both full and regular membership (see Table A.1 in Annex A).

The content of this report is based on the replies of national authorities to several questionnaires circulated across the OECD/INFE in recent years. Twelve countries directly replied to the Survey on Trends and Recent Developments in Financial Education in Europe (see Table B.1 in Annex B). Other sources include the Survey on the Implementation of National Strategies for Financial Education (2013 and 2014 updates), other OECD/INFE documents and publications (such as the joint Russia's G20 Presidency and OECD [2013] publication Advancing national strategies for financial education, the OECD [2014b] publication on Financial education for youth and the OECD/INFE [2015] Policy handbook on the implementation of national strategies), as well as desk research and bilateral contacts with countries.

The report also uses the preliminary results of the 2015 OECD/INFE survey on financial literacy and inclusion for European countries. The global and detailed results of the survey will be released in October 2016.

The overall content of the report was reviewed and approved by the OECD/INFE Technical Committee for publication at its meeting in September 2015 in Malaysia.

The structure of the report is as follows:

- Chapter 1 presents the main background issues and challenges providing a rationale for financial education in Europe;
- Chapter 2 discusses policy responses on financial education, including European Union policy responses on financial education, financial consumer protection and financial inclusion, as well as national responses such as national strategies for financial education and relevant financial education programmes;
- Chapter 3 concludes by providing policy and practical directions policy makers and other stakeholders.

Key findings

The report highlights a **number of factors and trends that spurred the development of financial education policies in Europe** in the last twenty years. These include population ageing and consequent pension reforms, increasing debt burden and households' vulnerability to over-indebtedness, growing complexity of the financial marketplace, and varying levels of financial exclusion, all happening in a context of **low financial literacy**, especially in some countries.

- Some European countries have taken action in order to address these issues. Out of the 48 European countries covered in this report, **over a third are developing, implementing or revising a national strategy**. Most national strategies aim at improving the financial literacy of their citizens as well as at supporting pension reforms, complementing financial consumer protection policies, and improving financial inclusion.
- Many European countries exploit a **variety of channels** (in the form of websites, online tools, information campaigns, financial literacy days/weeks, museums, etc.) to provide information on a range of financial issues that consumers may face at different points in their lives and to raise awareness on reforms impacting households' finances. Such broad financial education initiatives also provide information on the range of existing financial products and services, addressing especially people who are not fully included in formal financial markets or who are new to the market, because young or immigrant. These channels often complement consumer protection efforts in the form of financial product comparison tools.
- Moreover, **a number of financial education initiatives target more focused adult audiences**, often including vulnerable groups. These initiatives reach people at moments when they may need financial information, knowledge and skills on specific issues, such as planning skills for retirement for employees, debt management skills for over-indebted people (or at risk of becoming so), money management skills for low-income people accessing micro-finance, or greater financial awareness for newly arrived migrants.
- Finally, a great part of national efforts in terms of **financial education is devoted to children and young people**, and aims at equipping them – through schools or other channels – with knowledge and skills to face financial issues that they are likely to encounter immediately or in the near future.

The report also makes **some policy and practical recommendations** to support and complement the efforts already in place. These are in particular:

- **Design a national strategy on financial education** as a complement to financial consumer protection measures, following OECD/INFE guidelines, where this does not exist yet;
- **Collect and disseminate further evidence**, through surveys on adults' financial literacy as well as evaluation of the impact of financial education programmes, and develop research on effective delivery;
- **Establish solid governance mechanisms** to implement financial education policies backed by clear institutional mandates and to effectively co-ordinate all stakeholders; and
- **Strengthen delivery mechanisms**, by devising new innovative channels and by making sure all audiences are reached. Specific policy directions are provided for the introduction of financial education in schools, focusing on the need to mainstream teachers' training and on the assessment of students' financial literacy.

Chapter 1

Context and rationale for financial education in Europe

This chapter presents the factors that make financial education policies relevant in Europe: population ageing, household debt levels, the growing complexity of the financial marketplace and, in some countries, levels of financial exclusion. Against this background, the financial literacy of Europeans, in terms of knowledge, attitudes and behaviours, is still low. This is explained particularly through the analysis of the 2015 OECD/INFE survey of adults' financial literacy.

The development of financial education policies in Europe in the last twenty years has been spurred by a variety of interrelated factors including population ageing and consequent pension reforms, increasing debt burden and vulnerability to over-indebtedness, growing complexity of the financial marketplace, and financial exclusion, in a context of low financial literacy.

1.1 Population ageing and pensions reforms

Already at the beginning of the 1990s, western European countries that would then become part of the Euro area were among the oldest in the world. In 1990, the population aged 65 years and more was almost 14% of the overall population and almost 21% of the working age population on average in the countries of the EU-27; in 2014 the same figures increased to over 18% and over 27% respectively. During most of this period, Italy has had the oldest population, with an old-age dependency ratio of almost 33% in 2013 and projected to reach 40% in 2030. Germany, Sweden and Greece have also had high old-age dependency ratios in the last decades (Eurostat and World Bank, various years).

As a consequence, many European countries undertook significant pension reforms aiming at improving the sustainability of their pay-as-you-go systems. Most of these reforms led to lower replacement rates for younger generations (even though some recent reforms were aimed at ensuring adequate retirement benefits especially to the lowest incomes – European Commission, 2012; OECD, 2013) and led to a greater role of private pensions in many countries to supplement the less generous pay-as-you-go public benefits (Antolin, Payet and Yermo, 2012).

The growing coverage of private pensions and the progressive shift from defined benefit to defined contribution rules gave greater responsibility to the individuals (as opposed to governments or employers) in ensuring they have sufficient and adequate means to finance their retirement. These developments also revealed that many workers did not have the financial knowledge and skills to handle the increasing individual responsibility for planning and saving for retirement.

In **Denmark**, surveys have shown that many savers don't know which type of private pension they have and that they have limited knowledge of important characteristics of pensions' arrangements: A study by the Danish National Centre for Social Research showed that 11% do not know whether they have a labour-market or private pension scheme; another study of the attitude and knowledge of people living together with regard to pensions and life insurance showed that 58% of participants could not answer correctly to the meaning of the word "beneficiary" (Money and Pensions Panel, 2013). The **Netherlands** Pension Monitor in 2010 and 2012 confirmed that over 70% of employees do not know what their retirement income will be (Atkinson et al., 2015). An earlier study of **UK** adults aged 50–59 with a defined benefit pension showed that about 40% did not know the accrual rate of their defined benefit pension and that about 30% did not know how much pension income to expect upon retirement (Banks and Oldfield, 2007).

Based on the complexity of choices related to pensions' arrangements and on the lack of consumers' knowledge, many governments developed financial education tools and materials not only to improve the availability of information but also to help workers plan ahead and make choices regarding their retirement.

1.2 Household debt

In the period preceding the financial crisis, a number of factors reduced credit constraints on households and allowed credit expansion in Europe, including stable inflation, decreasing risk premiums, the development of the Single Market in financial services, higher and more differentiated credit supply, higher future-income expectations. The household debt-to-GDP ratio increased in the European Union until 2009 and then contracted (it was around 60% of GDP in 2013). Household debt-to-GDP in the United States followed a similar pattern (but started contracting in 2007 and remains now at a higher level – more than 80% of GDP in 2013). Low interest rates in recent years may encourage credit expansion again.

Similarly, consumer credit expanded before the crisis, undergoing a subsequent retrenchment. At its peak in 2009, consumer credit represented over 13% of household debt in the euro area (Chmelar 2013, Bouyon and Boeri, 2014). Figure 1.1 depicts the evolution of household debt in some selected European countries (data for more countries is available in Annex C).

Figure 1.1. **Household debt in selected European countries, 2004-2012**

Loans to household and non-profit institutions serving households as a % of GDP

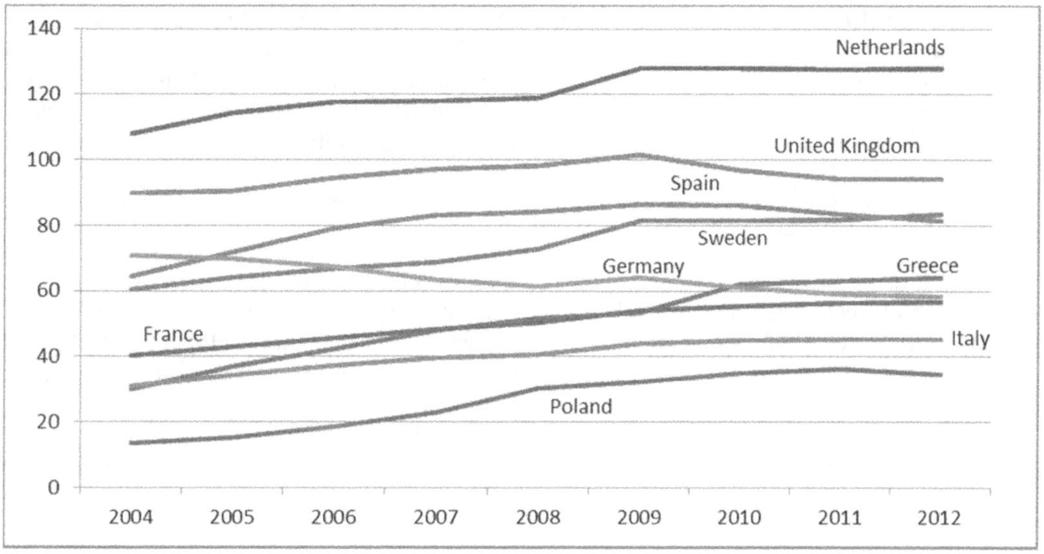

Source: Eurostat

Despite the decreasing average debt burden after the financial crisis, many households in European countries are still highly leveraged. Low-income indebted households are particularly vulnerable to economic shocks, meaning that an adverse shock to labour income or interest payments could lead to an unsustainable debt burden and economic distress (Eurosystem Household Finance and Consumption Network, 2013). A report commissioned by the Money Advice Service shed more light on patterns of over-indebtedness within the **United Kingdom**. The study reveals that across the United Kingdom approximately 8.8 million people are over-indebted (18% of the UK adult population), defined as individuals who have been at least three months behind with their bills in the last six months or have said that they feel their debts are a heavy burden. The report highlights that 64% of the over-indebted are women, 75% are below the age of 45, and they are characterized by different family situations as well as different levels of financial knowledge, skills, and attitudes (MAS, 2013a).

Another issue related to household borrowing has been the rise in foreign currency loans (mostly denominated in Swiss franc) in Austria and in some Eastern European countries, like Croatia, Hungary, Poland, Romania and Serbia. These loans were taken at times when interest rates in Switzerland were lower than domestic ones before the crisis but became difficult to repay when central European currencies depreciated against the franc in recent years. This also raised concerns that many customers did not understand (or were not sufficiently informed about) the currency risk related to these products (Yeşin, 2013 and The Economist, 2014).

Consumers' debt behaviour has been found to be related to financial literacy in various studies, including in some European countries (see Box 1.1) and governments in various countries have employed financial education together with debt advice to try to prevent over-indebtedness or mitigate its financial consequences for households.

Box 1.1. **Financial knowledge and consumer debt in the United Kingdom**

Two recent studies conducted in the United Kingdom show the relationship between financial knowledge and consumer credit behaviour. The first study uses 2010 survey data from a sample of UK households interviewed over the internet, and shows that individuals who borrow on consumer credit exhibit worse financial knowledge than those who do not. Borrowers with poor financial knowledge hold higher shares of high cost credit (such as home collected credit, mail order catalogue debt and payday loans) than those with higher knowledge, all else equal. The study also shows that individuals with poor financial knowledge are more likely to lack confidence when interpreting credit terms, and to exhibit confusion over financial concepts (Disney, and Gathergood, 2013).

Using the same sample of households, the second study finds that lack of self-control and low financial knowledge are positively associated with non-payment of consumer credit and self-reported excessive financial burdens of debt. Consumers who exhibit self-control problems are shown to make greater use of quick-access but high cost credit items such as store cards and payday loans. The study also finds a stronger role for lack of self-control than for low financial knowledge in explaining consumer over-indebtedness (Gathergood, 2012).

1.3 Growing complexity of financial marketplace

Many financial products and services can be rather complex, and consumers may not have the ability and willingness to collect all the necessary information for making an informed choice, especially consumers with low financial literacy and little past financial experience, such as young people, elderly, and migrants. As a result, consumers may acquire new financial products or services based on limited information (or on information coming only from the financial service provider).

Innovative financial products tend to increase access to financial markets and financial services, but may add to the complexity. Some innovative financial products can be particularly difficult to understand for some retail consumers, and may ultimately not be suitable for them (Lumpkin, 2010).

For instance, from the mid-1990s to the mid-2000s many developed European countries saw standard annuity mortgage being increasingly supplanted by mortgages with non-standard features, such as longer terms, or interest-only payments, or issued in a foreign currency. While such features aim at helping households to enter owner-occupation, these new mortgages can expose borrowers to greater interest rate risk or other economic shocks and are more complex to understand (Scanlon et al., 2008). Already in the early 2000s, the 'Miles review' highlighted the difficulties for many consumers to understand complex financial products, and especially mortgages, in the United Kingdom (Miles, 2004).

These developments have implications in terms of both financial consumer protection (in relation to product design, disclosure, selling practices and channels, and dispute resolution mechanisms) and financial education, as a minimum level of understanding is necessary to access new products and avoid mis-buying of unsuitable products by poorly informed or financially illiterate consumers.

1.4 Financial exclusion

There is a growing recognition globally and across Europe that having access to a bank account and other financial services, including credit facilities, is often a necessary condition for social inclusion. The access to banking (transaction banking services in particular) is seen as a universal need in most developed and cashless societies, including European countries. Lack of access to payment and transaction services can prevent access to other financial services (credit/savings), can make transactions more difficult and expensive for people who can only pay in cash, can increase the risk of being stolen, and can lead to time consuming and burdensome procedures, reinforcing stigma and exclusion (Atkinson and Messy, 2013).

Financial inclusion is high in some countries, especially Northern European ones, with financial inclusion rates nearing 100% and cashless transactions becoming increasingly common. In contrast, in several Eastern European countries more than half of the population does not have access to formal financial services. Owing to the low financial inclusion rate and high mobile penetration, M-Pesa mobile payments originally developed for Kenya have recently been launched in Romania. Figure 1.2 shows the increase in the percentage of adults holding a bank account between 2011 and 2014 in selected European countries. Annex D provides more extensive data on the percentage of adults holding other financial products across European countries.

The European Union legislation on a basic bank account[1] aims at improving access to basic financial services, but both supply- and demand-side barriers to financial inclusion[2] remain. In particular, lack of financial literacy is one of the demand side factors related to financial exclusion (see, for instance, Box 1.2). Financial education programmes can have a role in alleviating financial exclusion, especially among groups who have lower familiarity with financial products.

Figure 1.2 **Bank account holding in selected European countries, in 2011 and 2014**

Percentage of the population aged 15+ holding a given product

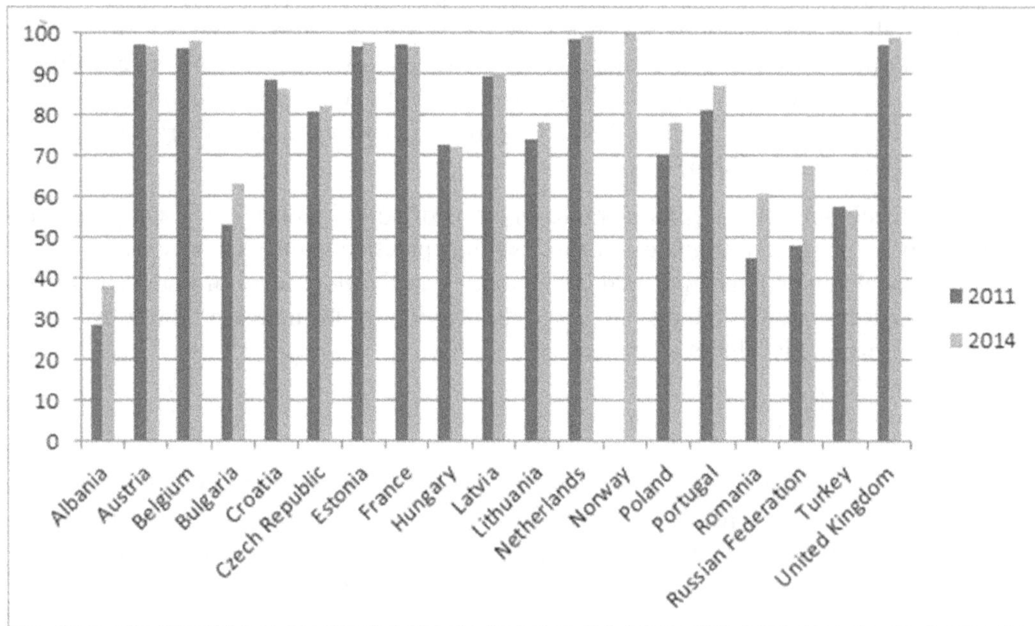

Sources: Demirguc-Kunt et al. (2012, 2015)

Box 1.2. **Demand-side barriers to financial inclusion in Russia**

In 2014 the Consultative Group to Assist the Poor (CGAP) conducted a qualitative and quantitative study on the demand-side of financial inclusion in Russia (Imaeva et al., 2014). The overall usage of financial services in Russia has not changed since a previous study conducted in 2011 (NAFI, 2012), with 23% of respondents reported not using any of formal financial services. The 2014 report showed a remarkable difference in financial service usage across income segments: 53% of respondents in the lowest income group reported that they are not using any formal financial services, while the same figure is less than half among on average across the country. A comparison of the two reports shows an important trend related to a higher use of credit than of savings products. This trend is especially pronounced among the lowest income people, whose use of savings products is five times lower than that of credit products.

The 2014 survey also showed that lack of financial understanding is one of the main barriers to greater financial inclusion. Insufficient knowledge about financial products ranked among the top five reasons for not using most types of products, except cash loans and credit cards. Not knowing enough about the product was mentioned as the second most important reason for not holding term deposits and savings account, after not having enough money. Qualitative research of financial literacy-related issues confirmed the available quantitative evidence on relatively low levels of financial literacy and reinforced the need to provide Russians with simpler and easier-to-understand financial products.

1.5 Low financial literacy

The factors mentioned so far provide by themselves a strong rationale for the development of financial education policies and programmes. The fact that they happen in a context of low financial literacy makes them even more salient. Several surveys in recent years have revealed the low financial literacy level of many Europeans, in terms of financial knowledge, attitudes and behaviour.

1.5.1 Financial knowledge

The increasing availability of internationally comparable evidence on financial knowledge allows policy makers and researchers to have a broader picture on the status of financial knowledge in the region. The analysis of data from the European countries that participated in the OECD/INFE survey on adults' financial literacy and inclusion in 2015 (the global and detailed results of the survey will be released in October 2016) provides cross-country comparable data on the financial knowledge and behaviours of their population (see Tables 1.1 and 1.2; see Annex E for the knowledge questions used in the survey; data collected during the OECD/INFE 2010 measurement in European countries can be found in Atkinson and Messy, 2012).

Overall, the comparison shows that:

- Most people appear to understand the concept of interest and correctly identified that none had been paid in the question posed.
- Across all participating countries and economies, the calculation of simple interest on savings posed a problem for at least one in four respondents (except in Estonia, the Netherlands and Norway where between 76.% and 80% of the population answered correctly), raising to over half the population in Albania and the Russian Federation.
- More worrying, with respect to compound interest, the large majority of the population cannot identify that the value of interest following 5 years of compounding would be more than five times the simple interest. The Netherlands and Norway stand out as exceptions, but still four in ten respondents do not understand the concept.
- The basic relationship between risk and return is more widely understood in every country; however an important proportion of the population could not answer correctly. In Albania, Croatia, Czech Republic, Lithuania, Netherlands, Poland, Russian Federation and the United Kingdom, the proportion of individuals who do not grasp this concept is above 20%.
- The concept of risk diversification appears to be even more challenging: over 30% of the population does not understand the concept in Albania, Austria, Belgium, Croatia, Czech Republic, Estonia, Hungary, Latvia, Netherlands, Norway, Poland, Russian Federation, and the United Kingdom.

These initial results from the OECD/INFE survey have implications for the design and delivery of financial education programmes. They demonstrate that Europeans, and depending on national circumstances specific target groups in particular, need support to understand and effectively make use of certain financial products. The lack of familiarity with compound interest can worsen or lead to over-indebtedness or result in irresponsible use of credit; while the lack of understanding of both the concept of compound interest and risk diversification can make the appropriate choices of long-term savings and investment products challenging, especially for more vulnerable sectors of the population, at a time when they may be critical to complement retirement income. See Box 1.3 for a further comparison of the financial literacy of young people in Europe.

Box 1.3. Financial literacy among 15-year-old students in Europe

For the first time in 2012, the OECD Programme for the International Student Assessment (PISA) measured the financial literacy of 15-year-old students. It assessed the extent to which students have the knowledge and skills that are essential to make financial decisions for their future. Out of the 18 participating countries and economies, 12 are in Europe: the Flemish Community of Belgium, Croatia, the Czech Republic, Estonia, France, Italy, Latvia, Poland, the Russian Federation, the Slovak Republic, Slovenia, and Spain.

Results from the PISA 2012 financial literacy assessment show that many students, including those living in countries that are high-performers in the main PISA assessment, need to improve their financial literacy. Figure 1.3 shows the distribution of proficiency levels among 15-year-old students in the participating European countries and economies. Students proficient at Level 1 on the PISA financial literacy scale display very basic financial literacy skills: they can identify common financial products and terms and interpret information relating to basic financial concepts, such as recognising the purpose of an invoice. On the contrary, students at Level 5 can successfully complete the most difficult items in this domain.

Figure 1.3. **Financial literacy proficiency levels among European 15-year-old students**

Percentage of students at the different levels of financial literacy proficiency

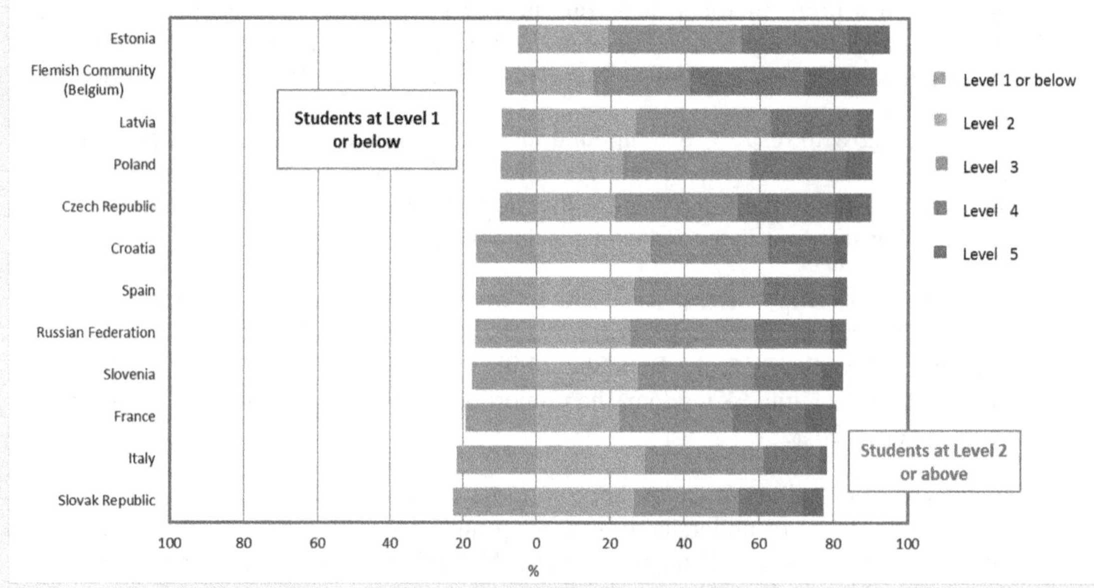

Note: Countries and economies are ranked in descending order of the percentage of students at Levels 2, 3, 4 or 5 in financial literacy.

Source: OECD (2014a), PISA 2012 Results: Students and Money: Financial Literacy Skills for the 21st Century. (Volume VI), PISA, OECD Publishing. http://dx.doi.org/10.1787/9789264208094-en.

Table 1.1. **Financial knowledge level in European countries participating to the OECD/INFE 2015 Measurement Exercise**

% of adults in each country replying correctly to a given question

	Interest paid on loan	Calculation of interest plus principal	Compound interest (and correct response to previous question)	Risk and return*	Definition of inflation	Diversification*
Albania	88%	48%	16%	77%	75%	65%
Austria	86%	68%	36%	86%	85%	62%
Belgium	91%	63%	39%	83%	80%	56%
Croatia	80%	62%	22%	69%	74%	66%
Czech Republic	83%	58%	22%	71%	73%	69%
Estonia	89%	79%	38%	85%	88%	65%
France	94%	57%	34%	87%	87%	75%
Hungary	91%	53%	24%	84%	89%	65%
Latvia	89%	72%	44%	82%	86%	64%
Lithuania	79%	68%	31%	75%	67%	75%
Netherlands	92%	76%	56%	73%	74%	53%
Norway	91%	80%	58%	86%	74%	59%
Poland	77%	61%	21%	77%	69%	56%
Portugal	87%	61%	30%	82%	87%	73%
Russian Federation	88%	48%	27%	78%	66%	41%
Turkey	84%	54%	19%	90%	84%	74%
United Kingdom	83%	57%	36%	74%	80%	52%
Total	87%	62%	32%	81%	79%	63%

*The percentage refers to correct answers to the main question where asked. The version with alternative wording was used in the Czech Republic (Risk and Return) and in Albania, Czech Republic and Lithuania (Diversification).

Source: OECD/INFE 2015 Measurement Exercise

1.5.2 Financial behaviour

The OECD/INFE financial literacy survey conducted in 2015 also provided a first set of comparable results on the main challenges in terms of financial behaviour in 17 European countries (see Table 1.2). It notably showed that:

- Over 40% of respondents had not gathered some information before choosing financial products in all participating countries but Austria, France and Portugal (where 66%, 80% and 82% do).
- Over 80% in all countries had chosen financial products *without* shopping around and using independent information or advice.

- Moreover, it highlighted that around or more than 60% of adults in Albania, Estonia, Hungary, Latvia, Poland and Portugal had not been actively saving in the previous year.

- On a similar note, more than half of respondents do not set long-term financial goals in all participating countries (except for Austria, Belgium, France, Lithuania and Portugal). This is especially worrying as this short-termism is displayed by a population that is ageing rapidly across all European countries, and for which ensuring long-term financial resilience and income will become of paramount importance.

- The percentage of the population that has borrowed to make ends meet in the previous twelve months is also high in a number of countries, ranging from over 20% (Albania, Latvia, Lithuania, Russian Federation, Turkey) to between 10% and 20% (Austria, Croatia, Czech Republic, Estonia, France, Hungary, Netherlands, Poland, Portugal).

Table 1.2. **Financial behaviours in European countries participating to the OECD/INFE 2015 Measurement Exercise**

% of adults in each country replying correctly to a given question

Country	Makes household financial decisions alone or with someone else	Household has a budget	Combined: Has budget responsibility and a budget	Active saver	Considered purchase	Timely bill payment	Keeps watch on financial affairs	Sets long-term financial goals	Some attempt to make informed decision	Shopped around and used independent info or advice	Income did not meet living costs at some point in previous 12 months	Percentage of the entire population that did not borrow to make ends meet in the last 12 months
Albania	83	71	60	43	95	81	75	41	53	3	54	59
Austria	95	31	29	69	79	88	87	65	66	12	16	89
Belgium	89	47	43	75	88	93	88	62	42	15	24	94
Croatia	88	70	63	63	62	61	63	45	33	5	35	80
Czech R.	90	40	39	59	76	81	75	39	30	6	18	87
Estonia	91	43	41	40	76	87	76	40	41	2	24	83
France	90	85	76	83	93	95	89	61	80	4	40	88
Hungary	94	25	24	27	75	77	56	43	21	6	26	89
Latvia	88	90	81	36	79	78	73	44	49	5	37	74
Lithuania	95	65	62	53	84	71	66	51	53	12	30	78
Netherlands	94	40	39	71	80	86	74	39	18	13	26	87
Norway	97	33	32	84	85	91	76	44	55	5	15	91
Poland	94	66	63	34	55	67	50	32	39	6	18	87
Portugal	93	72	68	37	93	81	79	52	82	6	35	84
Russian F.	93	50	47	55	72	70	66	47	52	11	35	76
Turkey	86	78	68	51	80	66	50	44	55	4	50	58
United Kingdom	96	53	51	72	69	84	75	45	36	15	23	93
Total	91	57	53	57	80	80	71	48	49	8	31	81

Source: OECD/INFE 2015 Measurement Exercise.

In addition to these first insights from the OECD/INFE 2015 survey, countries have conducted interesting national survey that can provide additional data to inform policy making.

Portugal conducted an independent survey of the financial literacy of its adult population (Banco de Portugal, 2011). The survey made it possible to identify areas and topics needing more prompt attention. A majority of respondents considered household budget planning to be "important" or "very important", but only about half reported saving, with only approximately 20% of respondents reporting saving in a medium to long-term perspective, suggesting the need of raising the awareness of the population concerning the importance of savings as a way of accumulating wealth to meet long-term objectives, and not only for immediate purposes. Moreover, when selecting products, few respondents (9%) indicated criteria related to costs or expected returns from bank products; in contrast, more respondents mentioned the recommendation from relatives and friends (35%) or practical aspects, such as the bank branch's proximity to their home or workplace (23%), as the most relevant methods for choosing products. These results are compatible with 74% of respondents indicating that they "don't know" or "know only approximately" the value of fees charged by banks on their accounts.

In 2013, the Money Advice Service conducted a survey of financial literacy in the **United Kingdom**, following trends on some aspects of financial knowledge and behaviour since 2006 (MAS, 2013b). The 2013 exercise revealed that more people are struggling with their finances than they were in 2006, with the share of people saying that they were struggling rising from a third in 2006 to over half in 2013. As a consequence, people are focussing more on the here and now than on planning for the future, including for unforeseen emergencies and paying into pensions and life insurance. However, most people try to cope and manage their finances: over 80% report to keep track of their finances (but only 47% make a personal budget); and the majority of people across the United Kingdom are continuing to save (but just over half the population save something each month, similarly to 2006).

Chapter 2

Policy responses to financial education needs in Europe

This chapter provides an overview of the financial education initiatives taken in Europe, in the European Union as well as at national levels. It focuses in particular on the national strategies for financial education implemented by European countries, and on their delivery of financial education to the general population and specific target groups (adults in need of retirement planning skills, the over-indebted or vulnerable; young people both in and out of school).

Various initiatives have been taken in the recent years, and especially after the financial crisis, to address the challenges outlines above. This section will first give an overview of the policy responses of the European Union in terms of financial consumer protection, financial inclusion (Section II.A) and financial education. Clearly, the European legislation does not cover all European countries and all aspects of financial education. The next sections will look more deeply at the national policy responses in terms of national strategies for financial education (Section II.B) and at various financial education programmes implemented nationally (Section II.C).

2.1 European Union policy responses on financial consumer protection, financial inclusion and financial education

In recent years, and especially in the wake of the 2007/2008 financial crisis, the European Union has significantly contributed to building a more robust financial consumer protection framework in Europe, including with the adoption of a number of Directives on credit instruments. The legislation on consumer protection in financial markets is also consistent with the G20/OECD High-level Principles on Financial Consumer Protection and the related follow-up work conducted by the G20/OECD Task Force on Financial Consumer Protection, of which the European Union is a member (G20/OECD, 2011 and 2013).

The European Parliament and the Council adopted in April 2008 a Directive (2008/48/EC) on credit agreements for consumers. The Consumer Credit Directive aims at improving consumer protection by focusing on transparency and consumer rights. It stipulates that a comprehensible set of information should be given to consumers in good time, before the contract is concluded and also as part of the credit agreement. In order to allow consumers to compare more easily the various offers and to better understand the information provided, creditors have to provide pre-contractual information in a standardised form (Standard European Consumer Credit Information), including standardised information on the Annual Percentage Rate of Charge ("APR"), representing the total cost of the credit. The Consumer Credit Directive also grants two essential rights to consumers, that is the right to withdraw from the credit agreement without giving any reason within a period of 14 days after the conclusion of the contract; and to repay their credit early at any time (upon a compensation to the creditor).

A report on the implementation of the Consumer Credit Directive released in 2014 highlighted that lenders should make further efforts to respect consumers' rights, especially in relation to advertisement and pre-contractual information, as creditors do not always inform consumers about their rights (European Commission, 2014).

In February 2014, the European Parliament and the Council adopted a Directive on credit agreements for consumers relating to residential immovable property (2014/17/EU), which Member States will have to transpose into national legislation by March 2016. The main provisions of the Mortgage Credit Directive include consumer information requirements, principle based rules and standards for the performance of services (e.g. conduct of business obligations, competence and knowledge requirements for staff), a consumer creditworthiness assessment obligation, provisions on early repayment, provisions on foreign currency loans, and provisions on tying practices.

The Mortgage Credit Directive contains an article on financial education, stating that Member States shall promote measures that support the education of consumers in relation to responsible borrowing and debt management, and in particular in relation to mortgage credit agreements. Clear and general information on the credit granting process is necessary to guide consumers, especially those who take out a mortgage for the first time, as well as information regarding the guidance that consumer organisations and national authorities may provide to consumers.

Financial consumer protection is to some extent also addressed by the Markets in Financial Instruments Directive (2004/39/EC – MiFID I), subsequently replaced by the MiFID II in June 2014. The MiFID I aimed at improving the competitiveness of EU financial markets by creating a single market for investment services. Additionally is also harmonised protection for investors in financial instruments (such as shares, bonds, derivatives and some structured products), by requesting financial institutions to assess customers' suitability for each type of investment product. MiFID II, which will be applicable starting from January 2017, aims, among the others, at improving the functioning of financial markets in light of the financial crisis and at reinforcing investor protection, including by strengthening the rules about conflict of interest prevention.

Moreover, the legislation on financial consumer protection has been recently complemented by a Directive aiming at improving financial inclusion. In July 2014 the European Council adopted the Directive on the comparability of fees related to payment accounts, payment account switching and access to payment accounts with basic features (2014/92/EU). The Directive stipulates that anyone legally residing in the EU has the right to open a basic payment account, and no-one can be denied this right on grounds of nationality or place of residence. This law also ensures that fees and rules for all payment accounts should be transparent and comparable, and makes it easier to switch to another payment account that offers better terms.

The Directive on Payment Services (PSD), and its 2015 revision (PSD2), are also to some extent relevant to financial education and financial consumer protection. In this respect, the PDS2 opens the EU payment market for companies offering 'account information services', that is internet-based visualisation services collecting information on different accounts held by an individual with one or more providers, enabling consumers to view their financial data in one place and potentially helping them to better manage their finances.

The work developed by the EU on financial education is more limited than the one on financial consumer protection and financial inclusion because the European Union does not have an exclusive or shared competence on education policy.[3] Nevertheless, the European Commission has been active in the promotion of financial education, for instance with the approval of a Communication on financial education in 2008 (COM(2007)808). This Communication underlines the Commission's support for the provision of financial education delivered to citizens by Member State, national and regional authorities, non-governmental agencies and the financial services sector. The Communication also presents some basic principles to guide providers of financial education, based on existing best practices. As part of the effort to promote financial education, the European Commission commissioned a stocktaking exercise of financial education programmes developed within Member States (Habschick et al., 2007), and enhanced the existing Dolceta online education tool to help teachers incorporating financial matters into the school curriculum (see section II.C.2.c).

2.2 National strategies for financial education

Many European countries addressed the challenges outlined in Section I by developing a national strategy for financial education.[4] Table 2.1 summarises the status of development of national strategies across European countries, showing that out of the 48 European countries covered in this report, 25 are planning, developing, implementing or revising a national strategy. Five countries – the Czech Republic, the Netherlands, the Slovak Republic, Spain, and the United Kingdom – have revised or are revising their first national strategy; twelve are implementing their first one; four are in the process of designing/ developing their first national strategy. Some countries – such as Germany and Switzerland – have not yet developed a national strategy notably due to their federal structure, while others such as Finland do not have a national strategy but have established high-level committees (in this case the Advisory Council on the Management of Personal Financial Affairs) aiming to improve the financial literacy of the population.

Table 2.1. **National Strategies for financial education in Europe**

Status of the national strategy (NS) for financial education	Number	Countries
A NS is being revised or a second NS is being implemented	5	The Czech Republic, the Netherlands, the Slovak Republic, Spain, and the United Kingdom
A (first) NS is being implemented	12	Armenia, Belgium, Croatia, Denmark, Estonia, Ireland, Latvia, Portugal, the Russian Federation, Slovenia, Sweden, and Turkey
A NS is being actively designed	4	France, Poland, Romania, and Serbia
A NS is being planned	4	Austria, Italy, Former Yugoslav Republic of Macedonia, and Ukraine

The following subsections give an overview of the approach taken by European countries at the main stages of the development of a national strategy.

2.2.1 Status of national strategies for financial education

Three countries – the Netherlands, Spain and the United Kingdom – have already revised their first national strategy.

- The National Strategy for Financial Education in the **Netherlands** was launched in June 2008 as the Money Wise Action Plan. The strategy was recently revised with a new timeframe spanning 2014-2018. The Ministry of Finance chairs a Steering Group that leads the national strategy. The Steering Group comprises the Central Bank, the Authority for Financial Markets, the Banking Association, the Insurers' Association, the Pension Federation and the National Institute for Family Finance Information (Nibud). A Program Board includes the ministries of Education and Social Affairs, the Consumer Authority, the Association of Financial Advisors and Tilburg University. A wider group (the MoneyWise Platform) including more than 40 partners from the financial sector, government, public information and consumer organisations, and the field of science is involved in the implementation of the strategy.

- **Spain** elaborated its first *Plan de Educación Financiera* (Financial Education Plan) in 2008 through an agreement between the central bank and the CNMV (*Comisión Nacional del Mercado de Valores*, the Spanish securities supervisor). The plan is managed by a working group where also the Ministry of Economy participates. The central bank and the CNMV revised the strategy and signed a new Plan for the period 2013-2017.
- The first **United Kingdom** strategy, "Financial Capability in the United Kingdom: Delivering Change", ran from 2006 to 2011 and was launched and overseen by the Financial Services Authority (FSA) which at that time was the body with statutory responsibility for consumer protection in financial markets. The UK parliament subsequently established an independent body to assume responsibility from the FSA for financial education, paving the way for the launch of the Money Advice Service (MAS) in 2011. The MAS launched a new Financial Capability Strategy for the United Kingdom in October 2015 (MAS, 2015).

One country, the Czech Republic, started revising its national strategy but the revision is not complete yet.

- The National Strategy for Financial Education of the **Czech Republic** was developed in 2010. It is managed by the Working Group on Financial Education, chaired by the ministry of finance. The ministry of finance and the working group started revising the strategy in 2015.

A group of another twelve countries are currently implementing their national strategies (Armenia, Belgium, Croatia, Denmark, Estonia, Ireland, Latvia, Portugal, Russian Federation, Slovenia, Sweden and Turkey).

- The National Strategy on Financial Education (NSFE) of **Armenia** was developed by a steering committee led by the Central Bank of Armenia. The NSFE was adopted by the central bank and the steering committee in 2013 and adopted by the government in 2014.
- The ministry of finance of **Croatia** led the National committee for financial literacy, composed by ministries, financial regulators, financial industry associations and others. The committee drafted the National strategic framework for financial literacy 2015 - 2020 and the Action plan for the implementation of measures in 2015. Both documents were adopted by the government in January 2015.
- In **Denmark** financial education activities are developed and coordinated at the national level by the Money and Pension Panel, a board established by the Danish Parliament in June 2007. The Danish Financial Supervision Authority (FSA) provides technical and analytical assistance and acts as the secretariat of the Panel.
- In **Estonia** the national strategy was approved in 2013 for the period until 2020. The national strategy was developed by a Steering Committee headed by the ministry of finance, and the implementation is coordinated by the Financial Supervision Authority.
- In **Ireland**, the National Steering Group on Financial Education was established by the then Financial Regulator (now Central Bank of Ireland) in late 2006. The Steering Group published a report 'Improving Financial Capability – a multi-stakeholder approach' in 2009, containing commitments and recommendations to foster financial

education in the country. Financial education activities are currently coordinated by the Competition and Consumer Protection Commission.[5]

- The national strategy for financial literacy of **Latvia** (2014-2020) was developed and is implemented under the coordination of the Financial and Capital Markets Commission (FCMC). A working group is set up to monitor the implementation of the strategy. The FCMC is responsible for coordination of activities carried out by the Working Group.
- The **Portuguese** National Plan for Financial Education (2011-2015) is conducted under the aegis of the National Council of Financial Supervisors, which is composed by the three financial regulators: Banco de Portugal; Portuguese Securities Market Commission; and Insurance and Pension Funds Supervisory Authority. It was approved in 2011 with the endorsement of the Minister of State and Finance.
- In the **Russian Federation**, the National Financial Literacy Strategy is developed as part of the National Financial Education and Financial Literacy Projected launched by the Russian Government with support from the World Bank in July 2011. The National Strategy is coordinated by the ministry of finance.
- In **Slovenia** the National Financial Education Programme was developed by an Inter-ministerial Working Group established by the government in 2009 and it was launched in 2010.
- The **Swedish** Financial Supervisory Authority created a network for financial education called Like Your Finances (Gilla Din Ekonomi/GDE) in 2010. The network develops and coordinates financial education initiatives in the country.
- **Turkey**'s Financial Access, Financial Education, Financial Consumer Protection Strategy and related action plans were developed under the aegis of the Financial Stability Committee and were approved by the Turkish Prime Minister in 2014. The Financial Stability Committee elaborated the Strategy through a holistic approach considering that the three aspects are interlinked. The Financial Education Action Plan (2014-2017) is coordinated by the Capital Markets Board (Turkish Government, 2014).

Other countries, including France, Poland, Romania, and Serbia are designing their national strategy. In **Austria**, the Ministry of Labour, Social Affairs and Consumer Protection and the Ministry of Science, Research and Economy are discussing the development of a national strategy. In **France**, a consultative committee released a report in 2015, commissioned by the French government, on the design of a national strategy. The report presents the results of a financial literacy measurement exercise, includes a stocktaking of existing financial education initiatives and makes proposals for the strategy development (CCFS, 2015).

2.2.2 The role of public authorities in the national strategies

Across the countries with a national strategy for financial education, public authorities are involved through different mechanisms. For instance, one public institution is mainly responsible for the development of the national strategy in Armenia (the Central Bank), Latvia (the Financial and Capital Markets Commission), the Netherlands (Ministry of Finance), Slovenia (the Government), Sweden (Swedish Financial Supervisory Authority), the Russian Federation (Ministry of Finance), Turkey (the Capital Markets Board), and the United Kingdom (the Money Advice Service). In contrast, more than one institution is jointly responsible for the development of the national strategy in the Czech Republic (the Ministry of Finance has responsibility in relation to financial education for adults, while the Ministry of Education, Youth and Sports is responsible for financial education in school), in Spain and in Portugal.

In some countries, the institutions responsible for the national strategy also have a specific mandate to develop financial education in the country. In **Denmark** the Money and Pension Panel was established by the Danish Parliament. In **Ireland**, the mandate of the Competition and Consumer Protection Commission includes providing information to consumers to help them make informed decisions, in particular relating to financial services.

In **Spain**, the role and responsibilities of main stakeholders involved in the national strategy respond to the functions assigned to each one by law or statutes. The Spanish Securities Markets Law 24/1988 states that the CNMV's function is to protect investors, and financial education is considered one of the essential complements to make this protection effective. The central bank main regulation does not foresee any specific duty related to consumer protection, but fostering financial education and literacy are considered a key tool for the promotion of financial system stability. The Ministry of Economy and Competitiveness coordinates the activities aimed at the promotion of financial education and financial literacy by royal decree.

The Capital Markets Board of **Turkey** was given the duty of coordinating the design and implementation of the national strategy and action plan on financial education by the Financial Stability Committee, which is chaired by the Deputy Prime Minister for Economic and Financial Affairs responsible for the Treasury.

Other institutions with a mandate for financial education include the Ministry of Finance in Croatia, the Ministry of Finance and Ministry of Education, Youth and Sports in the Czech Republic, the Financial and Capital Markets Commission in Latvia, and the National Bank of Serbia.

2.2.3 Direct and indirect involvement of private and not-for-profit stakeholders

To take into account the variety of (public and other) stakeholders with an interest and expertise in financial education, some countries have created collective bodies that are involved to various extents in the leadership and implementation of the national strategy. These bodies involve, depending on country circumstances and context, not-for-profit and private institutions alongside public ones.

For instance, in the **Czech Republic**, the Ministry of Finance chairs a Working Group on Financial Education, consisting of representatives of the government, professional associations, consumer associations, and experts in the area of education. The working group is a permanent platform for the sharing of experience and the coordination of key entities, institutions, and representatives of financial/educational projects in the country.

In the **Netherlands**, the MoneyWise Platform includes more than 40 partners from the financial sector, government, public information and consumer organisations that are involved in the implementation of the national strategy.

In **Spain**, the central bank and the financial regulator signed several collaboration agreements with banking industry associations, consumer associations, foundations, etc. to develop and promote awareness and educational programmes, to design and conduct a "training the trainers" programmes, to develop contents for the website managed by the financial supervisors, and to disseminate informative materials amongst their clients and staff.

The direct involvement of stakeholders from the financial sector in the provision of financial education has a number of advantages, such as the provision of resources and expertise, but can bring about coordination problems, and may generate conflicts between the educational and commercial activities of the financial institutions. Box 2.1 provides more details on the monitoring of financial education activities carried out by not-for-profit and private entities.

Box 2.1. **Monitoring not-for-profit and private stakeholders**

Given the growing involvement of not-for-profit and private stakeholders in financial education, some countries have developed sets of principles and guidelines to regulate their intervention and have accordingly devised mechanisms to monitor compliance with these principles. Based on the examples of European and other countries, the OECD/INFE developed Guidelines for private and not-for-profit stakeholders in financial education that were transmitted to the G20 in 2014.

In the **Czech Republic**, in March 2013 the Working Group on Financial Education approved the Principles of Independence. These principles are for voluntary use, but entities asking for a support and recognition from the Ministry of Finance have to fulfil the Principles.

In the **Netherlands**, MoneyWise created general guidelines for all initiatives related to the National Strategy, stating that they should be independent and non-commercial. More specific guidelines are provided on a case by case basis for each programme.

In **Portugal**, the National Council of Financial Supervisors published the "Principles for financial education initiatives within the framework of the National Plan for Financial Education" (National Council of Financial Supervisors, 2014). These principles aim at guiding the activities of entities engaging in financial education initiatives and establishing quality, accuracy, timeliness and impartiality criteria that must be followed by financial education programmes and materials. Moreover, financial education initiatives undertaken by financial institutions should be conducted under the aegis of their respective association. To be supported by the National Plan for Financial Education and to be disseminated via the Plan's website, initiatives must comply with the principles.

In **Slovenia**, all the interested stakeholders who meet the criteria set by the National Financial Education Programme (NFEP) can be involved in the creation of the NFEP and the implementation of different financial education programmes within the education schemes. The national financial education scheme can include all the programmes of interested stakeholders which are carried out in accordance with the principles and goals set out in the NFEP.

In **Spain**, as established in a series of collaboration agreements, private companies may submit materials to be used in the development of financial education activities. Whenever these materials follow the lines of the Plan and achieve appropriate quality standards, they are allowed to use of the logo of the national strategy (*finanzasparatodos*).

In **Ireland** and the **United Kingdom**, the financial sector is also indirectly involved in financial education through mandatory financial support. The financial education unit of the Competition and Consumer Protection Commission in Ireland is funded by a levy imposed on the financial services industry. In the United Kingdom, the Money Advice Service is paid for by a statutory levy on the financial services industry, raised through the Financial Conduct Authority. These funds are used to fulfil the statutory objectives, such as enhancing consumers' understanding and knowledge about financial matters (including the UK financial system), and enhancing people's ability to manage their own financial affairs.

2.2.4 Mapping, consultations and assessments

In most European countries that have a national strategy, the development of such a framework was typically carried out through mapping of already existing financial education providers and initiatives, and consultations with stakeholders, and through assessing population needs in terms of financial education by means of qualitative and quantitative surveys.

For instance, **Portugal** launched a public consultation among various organisations, including public entities (Ministry of Education, Ministry of Economy and Ministry of Social Security), financial sector associations, consumers associations, trade unions, universities, NGOs and other entities suited to the promotion of financial literacy. In the revision of its national strategy in 2013, the **United Kingdom** launched a call for evidence, supplemented by additional research and mapping work completed by an external consultancy.

While most countries developing a national strategy conducted some form of mapping exercise, not many evaluated the effectiveness of existing financial education initiatives. Even in the absence of formal evaluation, mapping and consultation exercises highlighted a number of issues deserving further action. First, in some countries, mapping and consultation exercises highlighted the importance of strengthened coordination among stakeholders, as they revealed that several financial education initiatives exist but that they are scattered and need to be better integrated in a coordinated framework. For instance, in **Turkey** it was observed that there were in fact many individual initiatives, but that each project could only reach a limited number of individuals and for relatively short periods because it was relying on limited resources. The revision of the national strategy in the **Netherlands** showed how over the duration of the first strategy, the existence of a national framework had dramatically increased the level of coordination between initiatives and stakeholders. In the **United Kingdom**, the mapping exercise highlighted the existence of a wide range of organisations currently involved in improving financial literacy in the country, but that there is limited sharing of best practice and evidence of what is having a beneficial impact, since delivery is not centrally co-ordinated.

Second, mapping and consultation exercises also highlighted the need to carefully define target group or re-define them in line with vulnerabilities across the population. For instance, in **Estonia** the mapping and consultation exercises revealed that some target groups received a lot of attention from many stakeholders (e.g. students in schools), while other areas were left uncovered. Similarly, in **Latvia** it appeared that most of financial education activities carried out by the competent authorities and market operators were addressed to children, pupils/students and teaching staff audiences as well as the general public, while there was a lack of targeted activities for specific at-risk groups, such as borrowers with money problems, the unemployed, indigent population, expectant mothers and mothers with young children, seniors/pensioners and so on.

Another major step in the development of a national strategy for financial education has been the assessment of the needs of the population in terms of financial literacy. Such assessments have been conducted through a variety of instruments, including national and international financial literacy measurement tools. Overall, surveys allowed the concerned countries to determine the level of financial literacy in the population and to identify priorities in terms of target groups with a greater need to improve their financial competencies and of specific aspects of financial knowledge attitudes or behaviour that need targeted action. These surveys also provide an important benchmark to monitor the evolution of financial literacy in the future and help evaluating the implementation of the national strategy.

Table 2.2. **Financial literacy assessments**

Country	OECD/INFE financial literacy survey	World Bank financial capability survey	PISA financial literacy	National financial literacy surveys
Albania	2011, 2015			
Armenia	2010	2012		2014
Azerbaijan		2009		
Belgium	2015		2012*, 2015*	
Bosnia and Herzegovina		2011		
Croatia	2015		2012	
Czech Republic	2010, 2015		2012	2007, 2010, 2015
Denmark				2013
Estonia	2010, 2015		2012	2012
Finland	2014			
France	2014		2012	2011
Germany	2010			
Hungary	2010, 2015			
Iceland	2011			
Ireland	2010			
Italy	2013		2012, 2015	2008, 2010, 2012
Latvia	2014, 2015		2012	2013
Lithuania	2012, 2015		2015	
Netherlands	2015		2015	2008, 2013
Norway	2010, 2015			
Poland	2010, 2015		2012, 2015	
Portugal	2015			2010
Russian Federation	2015	2008	2012, 2015	
Serbia	2012			
Slovak Republic			2012, 2015	
Slovenia			2012	
Spain			2012, 2015	2002, 2005, 2008
Sweden				2009, 2011
Switzerland				2013
Turkey	2015	2012		
United Kingdom	2010, 2015			2006, 2013

Note: *Flemish Community.

Table 2.2 summarises which countries have undertaken a nationally representative financial literacy assessment of the adult population and in which years. The table covers international survey instruments, such as the OECD/INFE financial literacy survey, the World Bank financial capability survey, the OECD PISA financial literacy assessment of 15-year-old students (OECD, 2014a), as well as national surveys (including national financial literacy surveys and/or household surveys investigating financial literacy, among other aspects). It also covers countries that have confirmed their participation in the 2015 OECD/INFE survey to measure the financial literacy and financial inclusion of adults.[6]

Table 2.2 shows that several countries have used multiple instruments in combination, that some of them carried out repeated surveys over time or plan to do so (in the case of the PISA financial literacy assessment), and that some countries have not yet measured the financial literacy assessment of their adult population.

Countries also used other instruments to learn more about the financial behaviour of households, including qualitative surveys, opinion polls and market research, consumer complaints data, reports from financial providers, financial market surveys, etc. In the **United Kingdom**, a nationally representative quantitative survey has been supplemented by ethnographic research looking at financial behaviours of families in the course of a year, with the aim to explore the influences on people's money management; identify and pilot test interventions based on those influences; and identify factors most likely to contribute to effective interventions. The study included an array of methodologies, including a literature review, pilot-stage interviews, four longitudinal ethnographic visits with 72 families across the United Kingdom over a nine month period, and 48 in-depth interviews with individuals who had recently experienced a significant life event with financial consequences (Elliott and Vlaev, 2014).

2.2.5 Policy priorities and target groups

As can be expected, most national strategies for financial education in Europe share the same goal of strengthening financial literacy, fostering responsible financial behaviour, and increasing financial resilience of individuals by improving their financial literacy.

In addition, some countries also defined other policy objectives, such as improving some specific financial behaviours. Given the proliferation and increased use of new and potentially risky credit products and the overall expansion of consumer credit in many countries, national strategies in Croatia, Estonia, France, Latvia, Netherlands, Portugal, Serbia, Turkey, and the United Kingdom specifically mention the need to reduce over-indebtedness. Moreover, following the long-term trend of pension reforms that involved most European countries and as a way to support domestic policies aimed at increasing national saving, many of them also aim at improving long-term saving behaviour, support recent pension reforms, and fostering saving habits in the population, including in Croatia, Latvia, the Netherlands, Portugal, Serbia, Spain, and Turkey.

In various countries financial education is explicitly considered a key element of financial consumer protection efforts (see also Box 2.2), such as in the Czech Republic, Portugal, the Russian Federation, Slovenia, Spain, and Turkey. Moreover, in countries such as Armenia, Croatia, Estonia, France, Portugal, Romania, and Turkey financial education is also supporting financial inclusion policies.

The definition of policy priorities is accompanied by the identification of key target groups of the national strategy. The national strategy coverage is typically quite comprehensive: many countries declare to target the whole population with a specific focus on some particular groups, or they target a combination of broad groups covering almost the entire population (such as young people, working age adults and the elderly).

Box 2.2. **Synergies between financial consumer protection and financial education policies**

In many of the European countries that have implemented a national strategy for financial education (hereafter in this box, national strategy), financial education is closely linked to financial consumer protection, at the institutional level and/or at the policy level.

In some countries, the national strategy is led (or co-led) by the financial authority responsible for financial supervision in the country and one of the goals of the national strategy is to support financial consumer protection efforts. For instance, in **Estonia**, the FSA conducts the supervision over banks and most other financial institutions and is strongly involved in the implementation of the national strategy. The **Danish** FSA supervises financial institutions to fulfil obligations according to consumer protection law and at the same time is the Secretariat of the Money and Pensions panel, which is coordinating financial education initiatives in the country. In **Portugal**, financial education is a component of the financial consumer protection policy conducted by the three Portuguese financial supervisors (Banco de Portugal, Portuguese Securities Market Commission and Insurance and Pension Funds Supervision Authority), which also lead the national strategy. In **Spain**, the objectives of the *Plan de Educación Financiera* are part of the larger goal of financial consumer protection. Financial education, together with supervision and regulation, is considered a basic pillar of consumer protection.

In other countries, there are explicit links between financial education and financial consumer protection policies. For instance, **Turkey** developed a consolidated strategy on Financial Inclusion, Financial Education and Financial Consumer Protection. Moreover, the action plan on financial education is planned to support the action plan on financial consumer protection and to enhance financial inclusion. In **Latvia**, the national strategy priorities are linked to National Development Plan and the strategic documents of various stakeholders, including the Financial and Capital Markets Commission, the Bank of Latvia, and the Consumer Rights Protection Centre.

Among the specific targets groups, the most popular is students and young people (including out of school youth in Portugal and Slovenia), as mentioned by Armenia, the Czech Republic, Denmark, Estonia, France, Latvia, Netherlands, Poland, Portugal, Romania, the Russian Federation, Serbia, Slovenia, Spain, Sweden, Turkey, and the United Kingdom. Alongside students, Estonia, Latvia, Slovenia, Sweden also mention teachers and educators among their targets (see section II.C.2 about financial education programmes for young people and about the provision of financial education in school).

Working-age adults are targeted for instance in the Czech Republic, Estonia, Latvia, Slovenia, Spain, Sweden, and the United Kingdom, typically with a focus on preparation for retirement. Other countries like Estonia, France, Poland, Romania, Turkey, Armenia, Denmark, the Netherlands, Serbia, target adults *de facto*, as they report to address individuals at particular life events or life stages. Estonia, Slovenia, Spain, Sweden, United Kingdom, France, Poland, Portugal, Romania, and Turkey also target retirees and elderly people more generally.

Several countries reported to address various groups of vulnerable people, such as:

- low-income people (Latvia, Portugal, Romania, Russian Federation, Serbia, Turkey);
- the unemployed (Latvia, Portugal, Serbia, Slovenia, Sweden);
- people in debt or over-indebted (Slovenia, Poland, Portugal – but de facto more countries aim at addressing over-indebted);

- migrants (Portugal, Spain, Sweden);
- women (Armenia, Poland, Turkey);
- people with low financial literacy (Latvia, Romania, Serbia);
- people living in rural areas (Armenia);
- SMEs and would-be entrepreneurs (Latvia, the Netherlands, Portugal, Romania, Serbia, and Turkey).

2.2.6 Evaluating the national strategy

Four European countries, the Czech Republic, the Netherlands, Spain, and the United Kingdom have reviewed or are reviewing their first national strategy. These exercises provide useful evidence and suggestions upon which other countries can build their strategies.

The evaluation of the national strategy in the **Netherlands** has involved an analysis of the MoneyWise platform conducted by an independent consultancy (Wijzer-in-geldzaken, 2014). The review notes the achievements of MoneyWise in creating a unique platform across the government, the business community and civil society organisations that enabled coordinated work. However, the review also highlights areas for improvement, mainly in relation to the cooperation between partners. The complex structure of the platform sometimes reduces the efficiency and effectiveness of the programmes. Conflicting interests within the platform can also lead to frictions and some partners interpret the role of the programme office (e.g., the body advising the steering group) differently. To address these problems, the review suggests the definition of a transparent and long-term structure for coopetition within the platform, where the programme office and steering committee take the initiative and set the parameters within which all partners can give their best contribution, working towards the overall objective of serving consumers' best interests. Following the revision process, the new national strategy also shifted to some extent its goals, from providing information, improving knowledge and raising awareness, to a greater focus on promoting responsible financial behaviour.

In **Spain**, the evaluation and review of the national strategy were explicitly included as a key step in the first financial education plan 2008-2012. One of the main achievements of the first Financial Education Plan was the introduction of financial education in schools, which was assessed by an independent expert. Overall, the results were very encouraging, as they showed that students' financial knowledge increased after the financial education courses and that teachers rated the quality of the materials as high, though they suggested a more interactive approach. Interestingly, the results also indicated that many school teachers involved would welcome an increase in financial education teaching time and they thought that financial education contents should be included in the school curriculum. The findings of this evaluation were incorporated in the programme for the school year 2012-2013.

In the **United Kingdom**, the development of the revised national strategy started from a call for evidence, asking for details of existing provision for financial education across the country. According to this exercise, almost 70% of organisations who responded to the call for evidence reported to have some form of monitoring or evaluation programme in place. However, most of these exercises consisted in process monitoring, measuring the number of people using a specific intervention, their satisfaction with the intervention, and the immediate or projected impact it would have on their money management, rather than actual impact evaluations. Only a few programmes asked individuals whether they had learned something new and how they would use it, but no evidence was reported about more objective forms of evaluation. One of the results of the call for evidence was the recognition that the use of different approaches to evaluation limited the ability to compare effectiveness of interventions and programmes. This was further exacerbated by different levels of resources available to each programme/organisation. As part of the revision process, a draft Financial Capability Strategy was published in September 2014, followed by a public consultation. 45 organisations provided a formal response, 16 provided an informal response, and further feedback was collected through consultation events. This was taken into account in the drafting of the revised 2015 Strategy (MAS, 2015). The Money Advice Service is also creating an evidence hub of evaluated financial education programmes (available at fincap.org.uk) and is planning to design a common evaluation framework that can be adopted by organisations delivering financial education interventions. These are expected to allow organisations to better understand what is working well and where further developments or investment may be needed in order to generate better outcomes for consumers.

Among the European countries that are implementing a national strategy, a variety of instruments is employed to evaluate the national strategy: some countries are using (or plan to use) repeated financial literacy surveys to monitor the progression of financial literacy in the population and assess the effectiveness of their initiatives, including Armenia, Portugal, Spain and the United Kingdom, while others rely mostly on the impact evaluation of specific programmes, such as for instance the Russian Federation. In this respect, Portugal noted that it is difficult to monitor and evaluate the initiatives developed by the stakeholders involved in the national strategy because not all stakeholders report all the initiatives undertaken and/or do not evaluate them.

Other countries in the implementation stage, such as Estonia, Latvia and Sweden, are planning a review/evaluation in 2015-2016.

2.3 Financial education programmes

Given the recent development of several financial education programmes within and outside the scope of national strategies, it would be hard to give a complete account of all financial education initiatives conducted in Europe.[7] This section therefore focuses on some selected examples of initiatives, mostly developed/initiated by public authorities, with a focus on innovative projects.

The review of programmes is grouped into programmes targeting a broad audience; programmes for adults; and programmes for young people and in school.

2.3.1 Programmes targeting a broad audience

Programmes targeting a relatively wide audience include websites and other online tools, public events (such as money, saving, or financial literacy 'days' or 'weeks'), as well as museums.

a. Websites and other online tools

Public authorities in most European countries have developed one (or more) websites with financial education and/or financial consumer protection content. Table 2.3 provides a summary of these websites and of the tools available online. They are often managed by a financial authority, but in the case of France the main financial education website is managed by a non-for-profit organisation. All of them contain information about financial products and services existing in the country and most of them provide information and directions about financial decisions and potential problems at key life stages. Some sites are quite comprehensive and address various topics and ages, while other are more focused. For instance, the website 'finansportalen.no' developed by the Norwegian Consumer Council, the Financial Supervisory Authority of Norway and the Ministry of Children, Equality and Social Inclusion has mainly a focus on financial products. Information is provided through videos in a small number of cases. Glossaries explaining financial terms and issues, and various types of calculators are also often included.

A few websites complement basic information with interactive tools, like comparative tables, games, quiz and applications for mobile phones. The Austrian central bank developed *Finanzcockpit* (finance cockpit) in 2013. It is an interactive online tool targeting students (16+) and adults. It seeks to increase financial knowledge and awareness, particularly in relation to risk, and it includes four different modules regarding financial decisions: Risk profile, Portfolio simulation, Stock exchange knowledge, and Risk and profit game/tests. In the Netherlands, the MoneyWise platform and the not-for-profit organisation Nibud developed an online tool called "What does it mean for me?". The tool gives people an overview of the impact of government measures on their personal situation, with actionable information. By filling in their personal situation, users receive an overview of measures that are important for them to know.

Some authorities are also using social media to reach young people and the general public. In Estonia, the FSA launched a Facebook account in October 2011. For instance, *Finanzas para todos* in Spain, MoneyWise in the Netherlands, and the Money Advice Service in the United Kingdom have Facebook, Twitter and Youtube accounts.

b. Awareness campaigns and events

In addition to websites and online tools, several authorities organise public events addressing a more or less wide target audience to increase the awareness of financial issues and provide information.

In the **Netherlands**, MoneyWise organises two annual events with a financial education focus: the National Money Week and Pension3Day. The National Money Week addresses primary school children and their parents. It takes the form of classroom training (accompanied by school materials, media events, etc.) on basic financial competencies conducted by over a hundred partner organisations. About half of Dutch schools participated in the last edition. The Pension3Day involves over 250 partner organizations to raise awareness of pension issues focusing on employers, employees and SMEs. In Portugal, the National Council of Financial Supervisors and other stakeholders organise an annual Financial Literacy Day every year on October 31 targeting the overall population and students. The event includes initiatives undertaken by stakeholders and the financial supervisors, such as conferences, workshops, debates, plays, games and other entertainment activities interacting with the public.

Table 2.3. **Selected financial education websites and online tools**

Country	**Website name**	**Info about financial products/ services**	**Glossary of financial terms**	**Info about life stages / events**	**Calculators**	**Tools to compare financial products**	**Games**	**Videos**	**Quiz**	**Other**
Armenia	abcfinance.am	Yes	Yes	Yes	Yes	Yes	Yes	Yes	Yes	
Austria	oenb.at/Ueber-Uns/Initiative-Finanzwissen/Interaktive-Anwendungen.html	Yes	Yes				Yes	Yes	Yes	Mobile app
Belgium	wikifin.be	Yes	Yes	Yes	Yes			Yes	Yes	Checklist
Czech Republic (CNB)	cnbprovsechny.cnb.cz	Yes	Yes	Yes			Yes	Yes	Yes	
Czech Republic (MoF)	psfv.cz	Yes	Yes		Yes					Tips and guides
Denmark	raadtilpenge.dk	Yes	Yes	Yes	Yes		Yes	Yes		Mobile app
Estonia	minuraha.ee	Yes	Yes	Yes	Yes	Yes	Yes			
France (financial authorities)	abe-infoservice.fr	Yes						Yes		
France (NGO)	lafinancepourtous.com	Yes	Yes	Yes	Yes			Yes	Yes	
Ireland	consumerhelp.ie	Yes		Yes	Yes	Yes				
Latvia	klientuskola.lv	Yes	Yes		Yes	Yes	Yes	Yes	Yes	Website optimised for mobile devices
Lithuania	pinigubite.lt	Yes		Yes	Yes			Yes		
Netherlands	wijzeringeldzaken.nl	Yes		Yes	Yes	Yes				Checklist
Norway	finansportalen.no	Yes				Yes				
Portugal	todoscontam.pt	Yes	Yes	Yes	Yes			Yes		
Serbia	tvojnovac.nbs.rs	Yes	Yes	Yes	Yes					
Slovak Republic	fininfo.sk	Yes	Yes		Yes				Yes	
Spain	finanzasparatodos.es	Yes	Yes	Yes	Yes		Yes			
Sweden	gilladinekonomi.se	Yes								
Switzerland	iconomix.ch	Yes	Yes					Yes		Simulator
United Kingdom	moneyadviceservice.org.uk	Yes	Yes	Yes	Yes	Yes				Chat
	21	**21**	**14**	**13**	**14**	**5**	**6**	**10**	**7**	**6**

In addition or in alternative to national events, some national authorities involved in the national strategy, such as Latvia (the Financial and Capital Markets Commission, Bank of Latvia, Ministry of Education), the Netherlands (MoneyWise), Portugal (Central bank, the Securities Market Commission, and others) and the United Kingdom (Money Advice Service), participate in the Global Money week coordinated by the not-for-profit organisation Child and Youth Finance International.

Similar initiatives are also conducted by the private sector. For instance, the Danish Bankers Association conducted the first national 'Money Week' 2014 targeting children from 13-15 year old and developed teaching material. The European Banking Federation organised the first and second European Money Week in March 2015 and 2016.

c. *Museums*

Many European central banks have museums dedicated to the history of money and the activities of the central bank itself. Some of these museums have a more explicit financial education connotation. For instance, the French central bank (*Banque de France*) is planning to open *the Cité de l'Économie et de la Monnaie* (the City of Economics and Money). The museum aims at presenting economic, monetary and financial notions and mechanisms in a playful, pedagogical and interactive way. The Bank of Latvia created a visitors' centre called 'Money World' with the aim of delivering financial education and information. In 2015 the Dutch Central Bank will open a new visitors' centre that will teach young people financial competencies through a series of interactive and innovative exhibitions. The *Museo del Risparmio* (Savings museum) in Turin, Italy - managed by one of the largest commercial banks in the country (Intesa-Sanpaolo) - has a similar educational and interactive approach. The Portuguese central bank opened a Money Museum currently presenting the history of money; a specific area dedicated to financial literacy is under development, with games and interactive tools for young people.

2.3.2 Programmes for adults

This section provides some examples of initiatives with a more targeted adult audience, such as employees, over-indebted people, the unemployed and migrants.

a. *Financial education for workers and for retirement planning*

Given the relevance of pension reforms in European countries, several financial education initiatives for adults have a retirement focus.[8] As mentioned above, the MoneyWise platform in the **Netherlands** organises every year a Pension3Day event, involving over 250 partner organizations to raise awareness on pension issues. The 2014 edition, for instance, targeted mainly salaried workers aged 30 to 55 to remind them that their pension is a relevant topic throughout their life and that they should regularly examine their situation and take action if necessary. The **United Kingdom** launched in November 2014 an information campaign about the State Pension scheme reform.[9] Other awareness and information initiatives targeted at workers with a focus on pensions take the form of websites offering information and calculators (see section II.C.1.a above), and personalised letters about the individual pension situation (see Antolín and Harrison, 2012 and Atkinson et al., 2012).

Other countries offer examples of financial education targeted at employees, but with a broader content going beyond just pensions. The FSA in **Estonia** conducted financial education trainings in the workplace in collaboration with human resources departments and their associations. The FSA also conducted two surveys (before and 2 months after the training) at one enterprise, which showed that that 32% of participants started saving afterward the training. In **Ireland**, 'Money skills for life' is a free one-hour personal finance talk, developed by the National Consumer Agency (NCA) to provide financial education to employees with the support of their employer. The talk covers six topics: Sorting out your money; Saving and investing; Insurance; Borrowing money; Dealing with debt; and Planning for later life. 'Money skills for life' can be organised as a once-off talk or as part of a series of employee development and welfare events. Talks are delivered by an NCA-trained presenter and each attendee gets a free handbook to take home, which contains useful information and tools to help them manage their money.

b. Financial education and advice against over-indebtedness

Debt advice services are offered in several European countries (Eurofound, 2011), and some of them combine debt counselling with financial education. The Money Advice Service in the **United Kingdom** provides free and impartial money advice through various channels (online, over the phone, in printed guides, and face-to-face). This recently included the development of a specific payday loan tool that helps users to find cheaper, lower risk alternatives to payday loans and helps them keeping repayment problems under control. Partner websites (including payday loan websites) link to the MAS tool. In **Bosnia and Herzegovina**, the not-for-profit organisation *U Plusu* (Association for Responsible Personal Finance Management Plus) provides free counselling and educational services in the domain of personal finance management to over-indebted citizens and organises tailored financial education workshops for adults and young people. The **French** association of bank users (AFUB) organises workshops for lawyers and social workers about the legislative and jurisprudential developments concerning credit and over-indebtedness. The central bank of **Lithuania** conducts a campaign with social media partners called "Be careful when borrowing (*Nepaslysk ant paskolos*)". The main goal of the initiative is to encourage residents to take borrowing decisions responsibly. The campaign involves the dissemination of information and the provision of advice, both for consumers who are considering borrowing, and for those who already have debt problems. Banco de Portugal is strongly involved in the prevention of over-indebtedness. Together with the Consumer Directorate General of the Ministry of Economy it makes information and education on this matter available as widely as possible, including training on preventing over-indebtedness situations and on the actions to take when it happens, as well as the dissemination of information online and on paper.

c. Financial education for vulnerable groups

Other financial education initiatives for adults target more specific groups of vulnerable people, such as the financially excluded, migrants, unemployed and other low income people.

Addressing financial exclusion through financial education is an important goal for several European countries. As mentioned above, **Turkey** developed an overall strategy covering at the same time financial inclusion, financial education and financial consumer protection. One of the goals of the financial education action plan was to raise knowledge and awareness about financial products and services as a way to strengthen the demand side of financial inclusion. Various initiatives listed in the financial education action plan have this overall goal (Turkish Government, 2014). Among other countries where the national strategy for financial education is meant to support financial inclusion policies, the **Portuguese** National Plan for Financial Education includes an objective to improve awareness of the basic bank account (Minimum Banking Services) that has been in place since 2000 and revised in 2012. In order to reinforce the dissemination of the basic banking services and promote financial inclusion, information on these services is publicised on the website todoscontam.pt and on the Bank Customer website clientebancario.bportugal.pt. Also, financial education lectures on basic banking services and household budget management are organized for trainers working in institutions that deal with vulnerable groups of the population.

Migrants are another important target group in some countries (Atkinson and Messy, 2015). The **Swedish** Financial Supervisory Authority developed a programme called "Your money your finances" that is designed to help teachers to work with personal financial issues with migrants. The material addresses Swedish economic terms, the Swedish banking and payment system, and clarifies rights and obligations in the financial marketplace in plain language. A film and a brochure are also distributed as teaching aids. Some non-profit organisations in the **United Kingdom** provide financial education programmes for vulnerable groups including migrants and their families, such as Citizens Advice Bureaux in England, Wales, as well as Advice NI and the Consumer Council in Northern Ireland (see also Atkinson and Messy [2015] for more details about financial education programmes for migrants).

Some countries have developed specific financial education programmes for the unemployed. The **Danish** Money and Pension Panel developed teaching materials on budgeting, loans and savings targeting young unemployed adults from 18-25 year old. The materials are developed for and distributed to all Danish 'jobcenters', where jobseekers look for jobs and get assistance and guidance on recruitment and the labour market. The Ministry of Labour, Family and Social Affairs in **Slovenia** carries out an experimental programme for social assistance, targeting at the same time unemployed and elderly people. As a part of the programme, unemployed individuals are trained to give assistance to elderly people in their fundamental financial needs.

As an example of programme for low-income people more generally, the Microfinance Centre in Poland delivers financial education programmes for low-income households across **Eastern Europe** and Central Asia. It has been organising classes on long-term financial planning, debt management, remittances, savings etc. as well as trainings for staff of microfinance and financial institutions since 2004 in various countries in the region (e.g. Azerbaijan, Armenia, Bosnia and Herzegovina, the Former Yugoslav Republic of Macedonia, Georgia, Moldova, Poland, Russia, Slovakia, and Ukraine).

2.3.3 Programmes for young people

Most European countries that have a national strategy for financial education indicated that young people and/or students are among the main target groups of their strategy. This is mirrored by a wide range of initiatives targeting young people, within and outside schools, including:

- The introduction of financial education in the formal school curriculum and the provision of financial education in school on a mandatory or voluntary basis;
- The development of pilot projects teaching financial education in schools;

- The development of teaching resources for school teachers and their professional development in financial education;
- The creation of other programmes and tools – not necessarily school-based – to address young people, such as social media, educational games and videos.

Only a few of these programmes have been formally evaluated. A summary of the results is reported in Box 2.4.

a. Financial education in school: mandatory provision through the national curriculum

Among all the financial education initiatives taken at the national level, the introduction of financial education in school through the formal school curriculum is the one that takes the greatest efforts. It requires the coordination and involvement of a wide range of agents (from education authorities to teachers and stakeholders in the private and not-for-profit sectors, depending on the country context), the definition of learning frameworks or learning outcomes, the development of teaching resources, the training of teachers and so on (OECD, 2014b).

This section covers countries where the provision of financial education is compulsory for at least some grades, or where it is planned to become compulsory. Such provision may or may not be developed as a part of the national strategy for financial education depending on countries.

In the **Czech Republic**, the introduction of financial education in schools started in 2007 with the definition of the Financial Literacy Standards, developed by the Working Group on Financial Education led by the Ministry of Finance. Subsequently, financial education has been made mandatory at upper secondary school level since 2009 and at primary and lower secondary school level since 2013. Before these dates, financial education had been delivered on a voluntary basis. Financial education is currently incorporated into various subjects: in primary and lower secondary school it is incorporated in mathematics, 'man and his world', civic education, 'man and the world of work'. In upper secondary schools, financial education is integrated in 'key entrepreneurial competency', mathematics, 'man and the world of work', social science, economics and other subjects.

In **Denmark**, financial education is part of the mathematics and social science's curriculum in lower secondary education ("Common Objectives") and its provision is compulsory. The contents of the Common Objectives are tested in the national examination in mathematics and social studies and also in the national test in mathematics. On the contrary, in upper secondary schools, where financial education is included in social studies, provision is not compulsory. An elective course in personal finance was also introduced in August 2014. This elective course contains the following core subjects: financial institutions and businesses, financial markets, income and consumption, life events and the need for financing, savings and investments. Similarly, the provision of financial education in upper secondary vocational schools is currently optional and part of elective courses. Schools can develop elective subjects that contain financial education, but according to the Ministry of Education, this is not a widespread tendency. However, as part of a reform of the Danish vocational education system, financial education will become a mandatory element of the first section of the new basic course from school year 2015/2016.

In **Estonia**, finance-related topics were incorporated to some extent in the first National Curriculum in 1996. The new curriculum adopted by the government in 2010 incorporates monetary and finance-related topics in primary and lower secondary school in a larger range of subjects. In primary and lower secondary school, monetary and finance-related cross-curricular topics are incorporated in human study, social studies, crafts and home economics, as well as mathematics. In general upper secondary schools, financial issues are taught in social studies and human studies under compulsory or elective courses. Schools must specify how they include cross-curricular topics into their classes. All learning outcomes of the National Curricula are evaluated in national exams and classroom examinations.

In **Ireland**, aspects of financial literacy are covered in lower secondary education in mathematics (mandatory), as well as in home economics and business studies (optional). In upper secondary education, aspects of financial literacy are also covered in mathematics, as well as the optional subjects of accounting, business, economics, and home economics. Students are assessed on financial literacy as part of the subject in which it is taught though classroom tests and national examinations/leaving certificates.

In **Spain**, a pilot programme was put into place for the first time during the academic year 2010/2011 and it was targeted at third year pupils of Compulsory Secondary Education (15 years old), with the collaboration of the Ministry of Education. The programme involved almost 3 000 students and 70 teachers from 32 schools. A minimum of ten hours were taught on basic personal finance concepts (savings, means of payment, responsible consumption, etc.). In addition, legislation was recently passed to introduce financial education contents in the school curriculum. The new education law recently passed in Spain (Organic Law 8/2013, for the improvement of the education quality) introduces financial education in the school curricula, both for primary and secondary schools. In primary school, education contents will be integrated in social sciences and children will learn basic concepts related to the value of money, saving, personal budget and responsible consumption. In secondary school, financial education contents would be integrated in economics, which is optional.

As in the **United Kingdom** education is a devolved function, financial education has been introduced in different moments and in different ways in schools in England, Scotland, Wales and Northern Ireland. From September 2014, finance education is compulsory within England's National Curriculum (taught in all maintained schools – publicly funded) as part of the subjects of mathematics and citizenship. Financial education is taught in mathematics in all key stages and in citizenship in Key stages 3 ad 4 (corresponding to ages 11-16). Financial education is compulsory for certain age groups in Northern Ireland and Scotland. In Northern Ireland, financial education is statutory as of 2010 for all students aged 4-14 years of age. An integrated-curriculum approach is recommended in which the aims of financial literacy are infused throughout the whole curriculum and all areas of learning are required to explore issues relating to economic awareness. At the primary level, financial literacy is taught mainly within mathematics but is also addressed, as appropriate, across the curriculum. At the secondary level, financial education is a statutory aspect of learning within mathematics and 'learning for life and work'. In Scotland, financial education has been a cross-curricular activity that all schools have been required to address from 2008 onwards. In Wales, the Literacy and Numeracy Framework became a statutory curriculum requirement for schools from September 2013. It is a curriculum planning tool that provides opportunities for developing numeracy skills – including money skills – across the curriculum and lays down the building blocks for financial education.

Box 2.3. **Kenyan soap opera as financial education teaching resource in the United Kingdom**

Makutano Junction is a Kenyan TV soap opera currently attracting over seven million viewers in Kenya alone. Eight series have now been produced and are being broadcast across Africa. Set in a fictional Kenyan village, the soap opera aims both to entertain and educate English-speaking African audiences. The storylines incorporate various educational messages in topics such as financial education, mental and physical health, and rights and responsibilities of good citizens.[10]

Thanks to funding from DFID (the UK government department responsible for administering overseas aid), the producers of Makutano Junction, Mediae, have teamed up with other British educational organisations and teachers to use Makutano Junction episodes to devise innovative teaching materials in subject areas covering social justice, human rights, youth and relationships. Materials suitable for Key Stages 3 and 4 (ages 11-16) are currently being developed to be used in a wide range of subject areas including Geography, English/Drama, Media Studies, ICT and Citizenship (where financial education has been integrated). Teachers and other stakeholders tested some of these newly developed resources with students in the South West, showing that they had a positive impact on changing students' perceptions about poverty, Africa and our global interdependency. The project is now being rolled out in Yorkshire / Humber and the North East.

b. Financial education in school through non-compulsory provision

Other European countries are at earlier stages of the introduction of financial education in compulsory education.

The Bank of **Italy** and the Italian Ministry of Education implemented an experimental programme to incorporate financial education into the school curricula starting in the school year 2008/2009. The programme was piloted in selected primary and secondary schools and has been extended to a larger number of schools and students in the following school years. Participation in the programme is voluntary, and financial education is introduced through a cross-curricular approach. Teachers who decide to participate receive training and pedagogical resources from Bank of Italy's officials, focusing in particular on money and transactions, and tailored to the needs of the different age groups.

In the **Netherlands**, basic financial education elements are included in primary education (money calculus) and in secondary education (household economics). After 2000, an increasing number of organizations started providing additional financial education materials to schools. Since 2008, a coordinated effort is being made with the provision of tested teaching material through the MoneyWise website, but their use is not mandatory.

In **Portugal**, financial education is integrated in the school curriculum in the area of citizenship education since the school year 2013/2014, although it is not a compulsory subject. It is compulsory for primary and lower secondary schools to offer citizenship education and to adopt (at least) some of its contents, which include financial education.

Also the **Russian Federation** is working to introduce financial education in schools. In 2013 the government developed core competencies for children that are then being used to develop financial literacy educational programmes. Educational resources also include teaching materials and materials for students, electronic modules, games and tests. At the same time some educational programmes for students have been developed and are currently being piloted in three regions, i.e. Kaliningrad, Tver and Volgograd.

Box 2.4. **Impact evaluation of financial education in school in Europe**

A growing number of studies conduct rigorous financial education impact assessments and show that there are effective ways of introducing financial education in schools. However, only a few of these studies evaluate programmes conducted in Europe. This box highlights the main results.

The Bank of Italy and the Ministry of Education launched a pilot project to teach financial education in primary and secondary Italian schools in 2008/2009 that was continued and extended in the following years. The pilot included an evaluation focused on students' knowledge and was undertaken through tests administered to pupils who participated in the pilot (no control group) before and after classroom teaching (Romagnoli and Trifilidis, 2013). Participants from the 2011/2012 school year could be split into two subsamples: those involved for the first time and those involved in the follow-up. Since the follow-up group had covered the core issue during the previous school year, results could be compared on students in the same grade who had been exposed once or twice to financial education. Indeed, the follow-up group showed significantly higher levels of knowledge than their coevals. As the tests were different from those of the previous edition, this was consistent with the fact that some of the information learned was retained after one year and it suggested the effectiveness of the programme in increasing students' knowledge.

Also the Bank of Spain evaluated its pilot introducing financial education in high schools for 15-year-old students as part of its national strategy. The study examines the impact of a 10-hour financial education programme in about 20 schools in the region of Madrid, using matched data on students' financial literacy scores, on the teachers who gave the course and on the family background. In the first part of the study, the authors compare students in school that participated in the programme with students in schools that did not, and find that the programme increased treated students' performance in overall financial literacy between one fourth and one third of a standard deviation. In the second part of the study, using also data from the PISA 2012 financial literacy assessment, the authors look at the factors that affect schools' propensity to volunteer to be part of the financial education programme (Hospido et al., 2015).

Another example of a financial education programme that was evaluated is an experimental study among 18-19 year old high school students in Italy conducted by Becchetti and Pisani (2012). The study covers about 3800 students in three cities. The programme offered a 16-hour extra-curricular course of financial education over three months. Difference-in-difference estimates show improved financial literacy in the treatment group after the course. The study, however, provides little description of the programme and no policy suggestions on what made it successful.

A fourth study reports the results of a field experiment evaluating the impact of a 90-minute financial education sessions on shopping, planning and saving delivered by the non-profit organisation My Finance Coach to 14-16 years old teenagers in high schools in Germany. Before the training, teenagers in treatment and control groups showed little interest in financial matters and low levels of self-assessed knowledge. After the training, treated teenagers exhibited a significant increase in both their interest in financial matters and in some dimensions of financial knowledge (e.g. their ability to assess risks correctly). Moreover, after the training, treated students showed a decrease in the prevalence of impulse purchases and an increase in intended savings in a hypothetical task (Luhrmann et al., 2012).

c. *Teaching resources and teachers' training*

Various countries developed financial education resources for school teachers, whether or not financial education is part of the national school curriculum, and whether or not financial education provision is mandatory. These resources are usually developed and tested by (or in collaboration with) educational authorities. They are ready to be used but, at the same time, quite flexible, so that teachers can decide how to integrate them in their classes. Such resources are often made available to teachers through online platforms. Some examples at the national level include:

- The **Danish** Money and Pension Panel developed the teaching material 'Funny Money' targeting children 13-15 year old on the topics of budgeting, savings and loans. The Panel developed the material in cooperation with the Danish association of Math Teachers. The material consists of short films and problems that the children have to solve. Furthermore, the Panel developed material (a video and print material) for parents. All the materials are available on the website 'Raadtilpenge.dk/funnymoney'.
- In **Estonia**, financial literacy study materials are available on the educational portal koolielu.ee ('School Life') since 2013. The total amount of compiled study material in Estonian language is about 250 pages (35 topics), for all school levels in different subject classes. Ten worksheets have been translated into Russian. Study materials consist of a general guide, a student worksheet and teacher materials. These materials were reviewed and financially supported by the Financial Supervision Authority, the Estonian Ministry of Education and Science, the Estonian Banking Association, and the NASDAQ OMX Tallinn.
- In **Ireland**, 'Money Matters' is a free resource that was developed by the National Consumer Agency (NCA), in consultation with Leaving Certificate Applied (LCA) teachers.[11] Its aim is to help LCA teachers and students to complete the units of the LCA Social Education course, 'Taking Charge', that relate specifically to personal finance education.
- In the **Netherlands**, tested materials from MoneyWise partners are offered to schools through the platform website 'www.wijzeringeldzaken.nl'.
- In **Spain**, the portal 'finanzasparatodos.es/gepeese ' was set up to give the teaching staff (i) teaching resources, guidelines and recommendations to teach financial education in the classroom, (ii) the curricular areas related to financial education, (iii) games, workshops, etc.
- In **Portugal**, teaching resources are regularly made available through the website *Todos Contam* (Everybody Counts), in an online library dedicated to teachers support. The three financial supervisors are also developing, in collaboration with the ministry of education and the four most representative industry associations, textbooks for the several stages of education, covering the main topics of the Core Competencies for Financial Education. Both the first manual targeting basic education students (6 to 9 years old) and a financial education e-learning platform (elearning.todoscontam.pt) were released in October 2015.
- In the **United Kingdom**, pfeg (Personal Finance Education Group) – now part of the charity Young Enterprise – developed resources and materials to teach financial education in school. It also developed a 'Quality Mark' indicating whether financial education resources aligned with national curriculum requirements and were of good quality.

Other examples of such platforms are 'unterrichtshilfe-finanzkompetenz.de' (*Unterrichtshilfe Finanzkompetenz* – Teaching materials for financial skills) developed by the German Federal Ministry for Family, Seniors, Women and Youth together with debt advice associations; 'naudasskola.lv' in Latvia; and 'iconomix.ch' in Switzerland.

The European commission created a website called Consumer Classroom (formerly called Dolceta - Development of Online Consumer Education Tools for Adults) to promote consumer education and in particular to encourage its teaching in European secondary schools. It is a multilingual pan European website financed by the General Directorate of Health and Consumers. The website puts together ready-to-use teaching resources on a wide range of consumer education themes, including also on financial education. It is suitable for teachers of students aged 12-18 but open to anyone willing to contribute. The website has been developed to make it easy for teachers to learn about consumer topics, create or choose ready-made lessons to teach their students and collaborate online with other teachers and classrooms around Europe.

- The availability of resources for teachers is sometimes accompanied by more formal financial education professional development for teachers. However, specific professional development is not usually available when financial education topics are not formally included in the national curriculum and the provision of financial education is not mandatory. In **Denmark**, social science teachers in primary and lower secondary school are trained to teach the students about the relationship between personal finances and political economy, students consumer behaviour, and to reflect on their own financial situation.
- In **Estonia**, initial teacher education is provided by universities and professional higher education institutions. This is aimed at developing teachers' professional and pedagogical competences including in cross-curricular financial topics.
- In **Portugal**, the teachers' training programme is based on a set of Core Competencies for Financial Education for schools and it was launched in 2014 by the three financial supervisors and the ministry of education. The training programme aims at supporting teachers in the introduction of financial education issues in the school curriculum, as part of Citizenship Education. Experts from the ministry of education and from the three financial supervisors are responsible for preparing the content and conducting the training sessions.

d. Reaching young people more generally

This section provides some examples of initiatives reaching young people through channels other than schools.

The Money and Pension Panel in **Denmark** launched in 2011 a Facebook page called 'Avoid petty debts' targeting young people 18-25 years old (www.facebook.com/paaroeven). The Panel also recently developed a free budgeting application for mobile phones (an 'app'), available at 'lommebudget.dk'. The app targets young people 18-25 years old and aims at helping them manage their expenses and not let the expenses exceed their income. The **Estonian** website 'Rahamaa.ee' contains, among the other content, a game for kids about money and saving.

The **Austrian** NGO 'Three Coins' developed a financial education game called Cure Runners. The game is designed to create 'transformational' rather than 'informative' learning (targeting behaviour rather than knowledge) and puts players in realistic financial situations (for instance players can experience bankruptcy and they cannot buy themselves out of trouble - many other games allow in-game purchases so that players can reset their status).

The **Italian** public broadcasting company (Rai Educational) in collaboration with the ministry of education and the Bank of Italy, developed a series of short financial education videos ("Moneyman" and “Money 2.0”). The project aims at disseminating basic concepts related to money and other payment instruments to young people in lower and upper secondary school through stories set in a day-to-day context.

Savings banks in seven European countries (**Austria, France, Germany, Italy, Luxembourg, Spain and Sweden**) developed partnerships with local schools and/or universities to jointly operate a financial education programme for 14-25 year old students. This initiative, called European Stock Market Learning, consists of the online management of a virtual portfolio of securities over a 10 week period to help youngsters understand economics and markets, and experience portfolio investment. More than 45 000 teams take part each year.

Chapter 3

Policy and practical directions for financial education in Europe

This chapter offers practical and policy suggestions to European policy makers to make financial education policies and programmes more effective and more beneficial to their citizens. The practical directions focus on the development of national strategies for financial education, the collection of further evidence, the need to have clear mandates and solid governance mechanisms in place, and finally on the strengthening of effective and fair delivery, particularly in schools.

This report provides an overview of the main issues motivating the development of financial education policies in Europe. Starting from these issues and challenges, the report describes the main trends in the development of national strategies and other financial education initiatives, with an overview of related financial consumer protection and financial inclusion policies where relevant. Based on the analysis of existing policies and programme, this section offers some policy suggestions to support effective delivery of financial education in Europe and thereby improving the financial literacy and financial well-being of European citizens.

Policy and practical directions

This section aims at offering some policy and practical suggestions based on the analysis conducted in Section II. As a complement to efforts already in place, more specific policy and practical directions can be suggested. In particular:

1. **Develop a national strategy for financial education** if one does not exist yet, in coordination with financial consumer protection and financial inclusion measures where relevant. These should take into account developments in the retail financial landscape, such as the impact of digital financial services. Countries can do so with the guidance provided by the OECD/INFE High-level Principles on National Strategy for Financial Education, and drawing on the lessons learned and case studies in the OECD/INFE Policy Handbook on National Strategies.
2. Continue to collect evidence, especially through:
    a. **Assessment** of financial literacy level and needs in the population at the national level, by using national or international instruments such as the OECD/INFE questionnaire for adults and the PISA financial literacy assessment for 15-year-old students; both surveys were repeated in 2015, and the PISA financial literacy assessment will be undertaken again in 2018. A first assessment can be useful to identify target groups and policy areas deserving more focused action. Repeated assessments over time are important to keep track of progress in terms of financial literacy and to ensure that revised programmes continue to be relevant in a context of changing social, economic and financial landscape.
    b. **Mapping** of the financial education initiatives being conducted in the country. This is a crucial stage in order to better plan a national strategy, if it does not exist yet, and if a national strategy or other coordinated framework already exists, to ensure that all groups in need are efficiently targeted, and that the relevant stakeholders are identified and involved.
    c. **Evaluation** of the efficacy and impact of financial education programmes. Several institutions monitor the implementation of their initiatives collecting information, for instance, on the number of participants and their satisfaction, but most programmes are not being evaluated (that is, to understand whether the programme is having the desired impact). Most impact evaluation evidence available globally comes from the United States or developing and emerging countries (under the impulse of donors and international organisations), but little evaluation evidence is available for Europe. Sharing evaluation results (for instance by translating them in English and making them available publicly or within the OECD/INFE) would also help all stakeholders

involved in identifying what delivery channels and implementation approaches are more effective in influencing financial behaviour.

d. **Research** about the financial literacy of consumers. Many aspects of financial literacy are still not sufficiently understood, including for instance the links between financial attitudes, knowledge and behaviour. Governments should continue to support academic research in the fields of consumers' financial behaviour, financial knowledge, personal and household finance, also as a way of refining their policies.

3. Build solid governance mechanisms, ensuring that:

   a. A public institution or coordinating body has a **mandate** to conduct financial education in the country, as a way to establish a clear leadership in the development and implementation of the national strategy;

   b. All stakeholders involved can and do successfully coordinate their activities, work towards the same objectives and avoid duplication of initiatives. If a national strategy does not exist yet and if public initiatives are limited, stakeholders within the private and not-for-profit sectors should try to coordinate among themselves;

   c. Whenever private and not-for-profit stakeholders are involved, there are mechanisms to avoid conflicts of interest and monitor their activities. Several European countries have successfully developed mechanisms to foster compliance with principles of quality, objectivity and distinction from commercial activities, providing useful examples to other countries. The OECD/INFE Guidelines for private and not-for-profit stakeholders in financial education offer an internationally relevant model to develop national guidelines.

4. Strengthen effective and fair implementation, for instance by:

   a. **Developing new and creative delivery methods,** by experimenting and evaluating innovative channels, such as games, interactive online tools and videos, especially to reach and engage young people. It is also important to combine innovative tools with well tested and evaluated traditional delivery methods;

   b. Reaching all relevant target groups, and especially vulnerable ones. In many European countries, social and financial inclusion is high in the policy agenda and most of them have adopted specific financial inclusion measures (including through the EU legislation). Moreover, several countries include vulnerable groups among the key targets of their national strategies for financial education, such as low-income people, the unemployed, over-indebted consumers, migrants, and, where relevant, also people living in rural areas and women. However, programmes targeting such groups are relatively less numerous and widespread than programmes targeting young people and the general public;

   c. Creating national events (such as financial literacy days or weeks) or participating in regional events (such as the Global Money Week and the European Money Week) can be a useful way to regularly raise awareness about relevant financial issues in the country.

5. Further strengthen the delivery of financial education in school by:

   a. **Mainstreaming teachers' training** on financial literacy within standard professional development programmes implemented by educational authorities. Teachers' training in financial education is sometimes left to voluntary and ad hoc initiatives developed by financial authorities, NGOs or the private sector, while it is important that teachers have access to both good teaching material and regular training within the scope of their professional development.

   b. Examining the financial literacy of students. Even when financial education topics are embedded in the curriculum, financial knowledge is sometimes assessed through classroom tests and national exams as part of the subject in which it is integrated, but it is rarely tested separately. At the least at the beginning of the introduction of financial education in schools, it may be valuable to examine financial literacy/education separately as a way to fine tune its provision.

Notes

1. Section II.A for more details.
2. The OECD/INFE defines financial inclusion as "the process of promoting affordable, timely and adequate access to a range of regulated financial products and services and broadening their use by all segments of society through the implementation of tailored existing and innovative approaches including financial awareness and education with a view to promote financial well-being as well as economic and social inclusion".
3. The Treaty on the Functioning of the European Union (TFEU) distinguishes between three types of legislative EU competence and draws up a list of the fields concerned in each case:
    - exclusive competences (Article 3 of the TFEU): the EU alone is able to legislate and adopt binding acts. Fields under exclusive EU competence include for instance monetary policy, customs union, and commercial policy.
    - shared competences (Article 4 of the TFEU): the EU and Member States are authorised to adopt binding acts in these fields. However, Member States may exercise their competence only in so far as the EU has not exercised, or has decided not to exercise, its own competence. Fields under shared competence include for instance the internal market, agriculture, and consumer protection.
    - supporting competences (Article 6 of the TFEU): the EU can only intervene to support, coordinate or complement the action of Member States. Consequently, it has no legislative power in these fields and may not interfere in the exercise of these competences reserved for Member States. Education policy falls under this type of competence.
4. See also the OECD/INFE High-level Principles on national strategies for financial education (OECD/INFE 2012a) as well as Grifoni and Messy (2012) and Russia's G20 Presidency and OECD (2013) for more details on national strategies for financial education.
5. The National Consumer Agency merged with the Competition Authority into the Competition and Consumer Protection Commission in 2014.
6. For more information on the 2015 OECD/INFE survey to measure the financial literacy and financial inclusion of adults please see: http://www.oecd.org/daf/fin/financial-education/2015finlitmeasurementexercise.htm
7. EIOPA (2011), European Banking Federation (2015) and Habschick et al. (2007) provide useful reviews.
8. See the chapter on financial education for retirement planning in the forthcoming OECD Pensions Outlook 2016 (www.oecd.org/finance/private-pensions/)
9. See www.gov.uk/yourstatepension
10. http://www.makutanojunction.org.uk/teachers-area/episode-summaries/series-1.html?phpMyAdmin=1fsBD3w5EHXJC4U4sqKUm1Rz7kc
11. For more information and to access the material see www.financialeducation.ie/index.jsp?p=895&n=909

References

Antolín,P. and D. Harrison (2012), "Annual DC Pension Statements and the Communications Challenge", *OECD Working Papers on Finance, Insurance and Private Pensions*, No. 19, OECD Publishing, Paris. http://dx.doi.org/10.1787/5k97gkd06kth-en

Antolin,P., S. Payet and J. Yermo (2012), "Coverage of Private Pension Systems: Evidence and Policy Options", *OECD Working Papers on Finance, Insurance and Private Pensions*, No. 20, OECD Publishing, Paris. http://dx.doi.org/10.1787/5k94d6gh2w6c-en

Atkinson, A., et al. (2015), "Financial Education for Long-term Savings and Investments: Review of Research and Literature", *OECD Working Papers on Finance, Insurance and Private Pensions*, No. 39, OECD Publishing, Paris. http://dx.doi.org/10.1787/5jrtgzfl6g9w-en

Atkinson, A. and F. Messy (2013), "Promoting Financial Inclusion through Financial Education: OECD/INFE Evidence, Policies and Practice", *OECD Working Papers on Finance, Insurance and Private Pensions*, No. 34, OECD Publishing, Paris. http://dx.doi.org/10.1787/5k3xz6m88smp-en

Atkinson, A. and F. Messy (2015), "Financial Education for Migrants and their Families", *OECD Working Papers on Finance, Insurance and Private Pensions*, No. 38, OECD Publishing, Paris. http://dx.doi.org/10.1787/5js4h5rw17vh-en

Atkinson,A. and F. Messy (2012), "Measuring Financial Literacy: Results of the OECD / International Network on Financial Education (INFE) Pilot Study", *OECD Working Papers on Finance, Insurance and Private Pensions*, No. 15, OECD Publishing, Paris. http://dx.doi.org/10.1787/5k9csfs90fr4-en

Atkinson,A., et al. (2012), "Lessons from National Pensions Communication Campaigns", *OECD Working Papers on Finance, Insurance and Private Pensions*, No. 18, OECD Publishing, Paris. http://dx.doi.org/10.1787/5k98xwz5z09v-en

Banco de Portugal (2011) Survey on the financial literacy of the Portuguese population 2010. Banco de Portugal http://clientebancario.bportugal.pt/pt-PT/Publicacoes/InqueritoLiteraciaFinanceira/Documents/Survey%20on%20the%20Financial%20Literacy%20of%20the%20Portuguese%20Population%20%282010%29%20-%20Final%20Report.pdf

Banks, J. and Z. Oldfield (2007), "Understanding Pensions: Cognitive Function, Numerical Ability and Retirement Saving", *Fiscal Studies*, 28 (2), pp. 143–170. http://onlinelibrary.wiley.com/doi/10.1111/j.1475-5890.2007.00052.x/abstract

Becchetti, L. and F. Pisani, 2011. "Financial education on secondary school students: The randomized experiment revisited." University of Rome Tor Vergata, Working paper 34, December 2011.

Bouyon Sylvain, and Filippo Boeri, (2014), Another contraction in European household credit markets. European Credit Research Institute statistics. www.ceps.be/book/another-contraction-european-household-credit-markets-key-findings-ecri-statistical-package

CCFS (Comité Consultatif du Secteur Financier), (2015), *La définition et la mise en œuvre d'une stratégie nationale en matière d'éducation financière*. Paris. www.economie.gouv.fr/files/files/PDF/rapport_strategie-nationale-d-education-financiere_2015.pdf

Chmelar, Ales (2013), "Household Debt and the European Crisis". European Credit Research Institute Research paper No. 13 (June 2013) www.ceps.eu/book/household-debt-and-european-crisis

Demirguc-Kunt, Asli and Leora Klapper, (2012), "Measuring Financial Inclusion: The Global Findex Database", World Bank Policy Research Paper 6025. http://data.worldbank.org/data-catalog/financial_inclusion

Demirguc-Kunt, Asli, Leora Klapper, Dorothe Singer, and Peter Van Oudheusden (2015). "The Global Findex Database 2014: Measuring Financial Inclusion around the World." Policy Research Working Paper 7255, World Bank, Washington, DC http://data.worldbank.org/data-catalog/financial_inclusion

Disney, Richard and John Gathergood, (2013) "Financial literacy and consumer credit portfolios", *Journal of Banking & Finance*, 37 (7), July 2013, pp. 2246-2254, http://dx.doi.org/10.1016/j.jbankfin.2013.01.013

EIOPA (European Insurance and Occupational Pensions Authority) (2011), *Report on Financial Literacy and Education Initiatives by Competent Authorities*. EIOPA-CCPFI-11/018 https://eiopa.europa.eu/Publications/Reports/Report_on_Financial_Literacy_and_Education__EIOPA-CCPFI-11-018_.pdf

Elliott, Antony and Ivo Vlaev, (2014) *Money Lives: the financial behaviour of the UK*. The Money Advice Service. https://www.moneyadviceservice.org.uk/files/money-lives-report-march-2014.pdf

Eurobarometer (2005), *Public Opinion in Europe on Financial Services, May 2005. Special Eurobarometer 230 / Wave 63.2*. http://ec.europa.eu/public_opinion/archives/ebs/ebs_230_en.pdf

Eurobarometer (2012), *Retail Financial Services Report. Special Eurobarometer 373 / Wave EB76.1, March 2012*. http://ec.europa.eu/internal_market/finservices-retail/docs/policy/eb_special_373-report_en.pdf

Eurofound (2011), *Household debt advisory services in the European Union*. Eurofound, Brussels. https://eurofound.europa.eu/sites/default/files/ef_files/pubdocs/2011/89/en/1/EF1189EN.pdf

European Banking Federation (2015) *Financial Education – National Strategies in Europe. Good Practices Report*. Published at the launch of the first European Money Week, March 2015. www.europeanmoneyweek.eu/wp-content/uploads/2015/03/GoodPracticesReport_EuropeanMoneyWeek-FINAL.pdf

European Commission (2012) *Pension Adequacy in the European Union 2010-2050*. Report prepared jointly by the Directorate-General for Employment, Social Affairs and Inclusion of the European Commission and the Social Protection Committee http://ec.europa.eu/social/BlobServlet?docId=7805&langId=en

European Commission, (2014), *Report from the Commission to the European Parliament and the Council on the implementation of Directive 2008/48/EC on credit agreements for consumers.* http://ec.europa.eu/consumers/archive/rights/docs/ccd_implementation_report_en.pdf

Eurostat (various years), Database. http://ec.europa.eu/eurostat/data/database

Eurosystem Household Finance and Consumption Network (2013) *The Eurosystem Household Finance and Consumption Survey: Results from the first wave*. European Central Bank Statistics Paper Series No. 2 / April 2013. www.ecb.europa.eu/pub/pdf/scpsps/ecbsp2.pdf

FKTK (Financial and Capital Market Commission of the Republic of Latvia) (2014) *Financial literacy: Latvia. Results of the financial literacy survey of Latvian residents.* June/July 2014.

G20/OECD (2011), *High-level Principles on Financial Consumer Protection.* www.oecd.org/daf/fin/financial-markets/48892010.pdf

G20/OECD (2013), *Update report on the work to support the implementation of the G20 High-level Principles on Financial Consumer Protection. Principles 4, 6 and 9.* www.oecd.org/daf/fin/financial-education/G20EffectiveApproachesFCP.pdf

García,N., et al. (2013), "Financial Education in Latin America and the Caribbean: Rationale, Overview and Way Forward", *OECD Working Papers on Finance, Insurance and Private Pensions*, No. 33, OECD Publishing, Paris. http://dx.doi.org/10.1787/5k41zq7hp6d0-en

Gathergood, John (2012) “Self-control, financial literacy and consumer over-indebtedness”, *Journal of Economic Psychology*, 33 (3), June 2012, pp. 590-602, http://dx.doi.org/10.1016/j.joep.2011.11.006

Grifoni,A. and F. Messy (2012), "Current Status of National Strategies for Financial Education: A Comparative Analysis and Relevant Practices", *OECD Working Papers on Finance, Insurance and Private Pensions*, No. 16, OECD Publishing, Paris. http://dx.doi.org/10.1787/5k9bcwct7xmn-en

Habschick, Marco, Britta Seidl, and Jan Evers (2007), *Survey of financial literacy schemes in the EU27.* Evers-Jung consulting, Hamburg, Germany. http://ec.europa.eu/internal_market/finservices-retail/docs/capability/report_survey_en.pdf

Hospido Laura, Ernesto Villanueva and Gema Zamarro (2015), “Finance for All: The impact of financial literacy training in compulsory secondary education in Spain”. Documentos de Trabajo. N.º 1502. 2015. Banco de España. http://www.bde.es/f/webbde/SES/Secciones/Publicaciones/PublicacionesSeriadas/DocumentosTrabajo/15/Fich/dt1502e.pdf

Imaeva, Guzelia, Irina Lobanova, and Olga Tomilova (2014), Financial Inclusion in Russia: The Demand-Side Perspective. CGAP, Moscow, August 2014 http://www.cgap.org/publications/financial-inclusion-russia-demand-side-perspective

Ipsos (2012) *Measuring Financial Literacy: Short overview of the survey results. Prepared for the needs of National Bank of Serbia.* www.financial-education.org/media/pdf/SERBIA_Measuring_Financial_Literacy_2012.pdf

Kempson, E., V. Perotti and K. Scott (2013), *Measuring financial capability: a new instrument and results from low- and middle-income countries*. International Bank for Reconstruction and Development / The World Bank. https://www.finlitedu.org/team-downloads/measurement/measuring-financial-capability-a-new-instrument-and-results-from-low-and-middle-income-countries.pdf

Klapper Leora, Annamaria Lusardi, and Georgios A. Panos (2013), "Financial literacy and its consequences: Evidence from Russia during the financial crisis", *Journal of Banking & Finance* 37 (2013) 3904–3923. www.sciencedirect.com/science/article/pii/S0378426613002847

Lührmann M., M. Serra-Garcia and J. Winter, (2012), "The effects of financial literacy training: Evidence from a field experiment with German high-school children", University of Munich Discussion Paper No. 2012-24, http://epub.ub.uni-muenchen.de/14101/

Stephen Lumpkin (2010), "Consumer Protection and Financial Innovation: A Few Basic Propositions", *OECD Journal: Financial Market Trends*, Vol. 2010/1. http://dx.doi.org/10.1787/fmt-2010-5km7k9tp2jxv

MAS (Money Advice Service) (2013a), *Indebted lives: the complexities of life in debt*. The Money Advice Service, London (November 2013). https://www.moneyadviceservice.org.uk/en/static/indebted-lives-the-complexities-of-life-in-debt-press-office

MAS (Money Advice Service) (2013b), *The Financial Capability of the UK*. The Money Advice Service, London (November 2013) https://www.moneyadviceservice.org.uk/en/static/the-financial-capability-of-the-uk

MAS (Money Advice Service) (2015), The Financial Capability Strategy for the UK, London (October 2015) www.fincap.org.uk/uk_strategy

Messy,F. and C. Monticone (2012), "The Status of Financial Education in Africa", *OECD Working Papers on Finance, Insurance and Private Pensions*, No. 25, OECD Publishing, Paris. http://dx.doi.org/10.1787/5k94cqqx90wl-en

Messy,F. and C. Monticone (2016), "Financial Education Policies in Asia and the Pacific", *OECD Working Papers on Finance, Insurance and Private Pensions*, No. 40, OECD Publishing, Paris. http://dx.doi.org/10.1787/5jm5b32v5vvc-en

Miles, David (2004), *The UK Mortgage Market: Taking a Longer-Term View. Final Report and Recommendations*, March 2004. HM Treasury, UK.

Money and Pensions Panel (2013), *Basic pension: the default option for labour-market pensions*. Report by the Committee of the Money and Pension Panel. February 2013. www.raadtilpenge.dk/~/media/PPP/Pensionsrapport/Basic%20pension_full%20report.ashx

NAFI (National Agency for Financial Studies) (2012), *One Hundred Facts on the Financial Behavior of Russians*. Moscow: NAFI.

National Council of Financial Supervisors, (2014). *Portuguese National Plan for Financial Education: Principles for Financial Education Initiatives.* www.todoscontam.pt/SiteCollectionDocuments/PrinciplesFinancialEducationInitiatives.pdf

OECD. (2013), *Pensions at a Glance 2013: OECD and G20 Indicators*, OECD Publishing, Paris. http://dx.doi.org/10.1787/pension_glance-2013-en

OECD. (2014), *PISA 2012 Results: Students and Money (Volume VI): Financial Literacy Skills for the 21st Century*, PISA, OECD Publishing, Paris. http://dx.doi.org/10.1787/9789264208094-en

OECD. (2014), *Financial Education for Youth: The Role of Schools*, OECD Publishing, Paris. http://dx.doi.org/10.1787/9789264174825-en

OECD/INFE (2012a), *High-level Principles on National Strategies for Financial Education.* http://www.oecd.org/daf/fin/financial-education/OECD_INFE_High_Level_Principles_National_Strategies_Financial_Education_APEC.pdf

OECD/INFE (2012b), *High-level principles for the evaluation of financial education programmes.* www.oecd.org/daf/fin/financial-education/49373959.pdf

OECD/INFE (2014) *Guidelines for private and not-for-profit stakeholders in financial education.* www.oecd.org/daf/fin/financial-education/guidelines-private-not-for-profit-financial-education.pdf

OECD/INFE (2015a), *2015 OECD/INFE Toolkit to measure financial literacy and financial inclusion.* www.oecd.org/daf/fin/financial-education/2015_OECD_INFE_Toolkit_Measuring_Financial_Literacy.pdf

OECD/INFE (2015b), *National Strategies for Financial Education: OECD/INFE Policy Handbook.* http://www.oecd.org/daf/fin/financial-education/national-strategies-for-financial-education-policy-handbook.htm

Romagnoli A. and Trifilidis M. (2013), "Does financial education at school work? Evidence from Italy", *Occasional Papers (Questioni di Economia e Finanza),* No 155, Bank of Italy Publishing.

Russia's G20 Presidency and OECD (2013), *Advancing national Strategies for Financial Education.* www.oecd.org/finance/financial-education/advancing-national-strategies-for-financial-education.htm

Scanlon Kathleen, Jens Lunde & Christine Whitehead (2008) "Mortgage Product Innovation in Advanced Economies: More Choice, More Risk", *International Journal of Housing Policy*, 8:2, 109-131 http://dx.doi.org/10.1080/14616710802037359

The Economist (2014), Forint exchange. Hungary's government gives struggling borrowers a break. 15 November 2014. www.economist.com/news/finance-and-economics/21632651-hungarys-government-gives-struggling-borrowers-break-forint-exchange

Turkish Government, (2014), *Financial Access, Financial Education, Financial Consumer Protection Strategy and Action Plans.* https://hazine.gov.tr/File/?path=ROOT%2FDocuments%2FGeneral+Content%2FFinancial+Inclusion.pdf

Università Cattolica del Sacro Cuore, Università di Milano Bicocca, Invalsi, Consorzio PattiChiari (eds.) (2014) *Le competenze economico-finanziarie degli Italiani.* www.economiascuola.it/ricerche-edufin/competenza-fin-2014

Wijzer-in-geldzaken, (2013) *Publieksmonitor*, www.wijzeringeldzaken.nl/media/994131/publieksmonitor-2013_wijzer-in-geldzaken.pdf

Wijzer-in-geldzaken, (2014) *National Strategy for Financial Education in the Netherlands 2014 – 2018.* www.wijzeringeldzaken.nl/media/1036345/7158-wig-strategic%20programme-web_eng.pdf

World Bank (various years), *World Development Indicators*, World Bank, Washington, DC. http://data.worldbank.org/data-catalog/world-development-indicators

Yeşin, Pınar (2013) *Foreign Currency Loans and Systemic Risk in Europe*. Federal Reserve Bank of St. Louis Review, May/June 2013 https://research.stlouisfed.org/publications/review/13/03/219-236Yesin.pdf

Annex A

Definition of Europe and OECD/INFE membership in Europe

This report adopts a broad definition of Europe, based on both the United Nations definition and on membership of the Council of Europe (that is, Armenia, Azerbaijan, Cyprus[1], Georgia and Turkey are members of the Council of Europe but are not included in the UN definition of Europe). This definition includes all members of the European Union, as well as 24 members of the OECD (out of 34).

The countries covered in this report are: Albania, Andorra, Armenia, Austria, Azerbaijan, Belarus, Belgium, Bosnia and Herzegovina, Bulgaria, Croatia, Cyprus, Czech Republic, Denmark, Estonia, Finland, the Former Yugoslav Republic of Macedonia, France, Georgia, Germany, Greece, Hungary, Iceland, Ireland, Italy, Latvia, Liechtenstein, Lithuania, Luxembourg, Malta, Monaco, Montenegro, Netherlands, Norway, Poland, Portugal, Republic of Moldova, Romania, Russian Federation, San Marino, Serbia, Slovak Republic, Slovenia, Spain, Sweden, Switzerland, Turkey, Ukraine, and United Kingdom (48 countries).

Table A.1 details the OECD/INFE membership status of the European countries covered in this report.

Table A.1. **OECD/INFE membership in Europe**

INFE membership	Number	Countries
Countries that have both full and regular member(s)	20	Albania, Armenia, Austria, Bosnia and Herzegovina, Czech Republic, Estonia, France, Germany, Hungary, Ireland, Italy, Norway, Poland, Romania, Russian Federation, Slovak Republic, Switzerland, Turkey, Ukraine, United Kingdom
Countries that have full member(s) but no regular member(s)	10	Belgium, Denmark, the Former Yugoslav Republic of Macedonia Latvia, Lithuania, Luxembourg, Netherlands, Portugal, Serbia, Spain,
Countries that only have regular member(s)	10	Azerbaijan, Belarus, Bulgaria, Croatia, Finland, Greece, Iceland, Malta, Slovenia, Sweden
Countries with neither full nor regular members	8	Andorra, Cyprus, Georgia, Liechtenstein, Monaco, Montenegro, Republic of Moldova, San Marino

1. Note by Turkey: The information in this document with reference to "Cyprus" relates to the southern part of the Island. There is no single authority representing both Turkish and Greek Cypriot people on the Island. Turkey recognises the Turkish Republic of Northern Cyprus (TRNC). Until a lasting and equitable solution is found within the context of the United Nations, Turkey shall preserve its position concerning the "Cyprus issue".

Note by all the European Union Member States of the OECD and the European Union: The Republic of Cyprus is recognised by all members of the United Nations with the exception of Turkey. The information in this document relates to the area under the effective control of the Government of the Republic of Cyprus.

Annex B

Sources of information by country

Table B.1 reports which European countries have replied to recent OECD/INFE questionnaires.

Table B.1. **Sources of information by country**

Countries that replied to the Survey on Trends and Recent Developments in Financial Education in Europe	European countries that replied to the Survey on the Implementation of National Strategies for Financial Education (or previous surveys on National Strategies)
	Armenia
	Austria
	Croatia
Czech Republic	Czech Republic
Denmark	Denmark
Estonia	Estonia
Former Yugoslav Republic of Macedonia	
	France
	Germany
	Ireland
	Italy
Latvia	Latvia
Luxembourg	Luxembourg
Netherlands	Netherlands
	Poland
Portugal	Portugal
	Romania
	Russian Federation
	Serbia
	Slovak Republic
	Slovenia
Spain	Spain
Sweden	Sweden
Switzerland	
	Turkey
	Ukraine
United Kingdom	United Kingdom

Annex C

Household debt data

Table C.1. **Household debt**

Loans to household and non-profit institutions serving households as a % of GDP

	2004	2005	2006	2007	2008	2009	2010	2011	2012
Belgium	40.4	43.0	45.1	46.7	49.2	51.6	52.7	54.4	55.8
Bulgaria	11.1	15.3	17.9	23.0	26.7	28.7	27.5	25.5	24.4
Czech Republic	14.3	17.1	19.8	24.2	26.8	29.6	30.1	31.5	32.4
Denmark	108.4	116.2	121.4	128.7	132.2	145.5	140.5	140.6	139.7
Germany	70.9	69.9	67.3	63.3	61.5	63.9	61.0	58.9	58.2
Estonia	24.2	32.3	42.3	47.0	51.4	57.7	54.1	47.0	43.1
Ireland	73.0	86.3	95.3	102.5	112.5	121.8	116.9	109.9	105.1
Greece	29.8	36.8	42.4	48.0	51.7	53.3	62.1	63.2	63.9
Spain	64.4	71.9	79.2	83.2	84.0	86.6	86.2	83.6	81.3
France	40.2	43.1	45.6	48.2	50.2	54.0	55.4	56.3	56.7
Croatia	27.9	31.1	34.9	37.9	39.3	40.3	42.5	42.0	41.6
Italy	31.0	34.2	37.1	39.5	40.5	44.0	45.1	45.4	45.3
Latvia	13.7	21.8	31.4	33.7	32.7	36.1	34.2	28.4	24.5
Lithuania	9.0	13.8	20.5	26.8	28.7	33.0	30.0	26.1	24.0
Luxembourg					49.3	55.6	53.9	55.0	56.8
Hungary	19.9	23.5	26.2	30.2	36.7	38.2	40.0	37.8	32.0
Malta	43.0	46.1	50.6	53.4	55.5	61.3	60.2	61.1	61.9
Netherlands	107.8	114.1	117.6	118.1	119.1	127.9	128.0	127.7	127.9
Austria	50.7	54.1	54.5	53.8	54.6	56.1	57.0	55.6	54.5
Poland	13.4	15.1	18.5	22.9	30.3	32.2	34.8	36.1	34.7
Portugal	76.9	81.9	86.3	88.8	91.8	95.4	94.0	92.7	91.6
Romania	6.3	9.9	13.3	18.7	21.4	22.6	23.0	21.8	20.9
Slovenia	16.5	19.1	21.8	24.9	26.1	29.1	31.0	30.6	30.5
Slovakia	8.3	12.6	14.4	18.5	21.6	24.3	25.6	27.0	28.3
Finland	43.2	47.9	51.3	52.6	54.7	61.9	63.4	63.5	65.4
Sweden	60.3	64.1	66.8	68.9	72.7	81.3	81.3	81.9	83.6
United Kingdom	89.8	90.6	94.6	97.2	98.3	101.4	96.9	94.3	94.2
Iceland	95.8	107.1	113.6	119.2	100.0	105.9	99.7	95.0	95.9
Norway	68.8	69.9	71.2	75.1	72.8	83.1	83.4	82.8	84.4
Switzerland	116.9	118.9	117.1	113.3	109.9	116.6	118.2	120.7	124.1

Source: Eurostat

Annex D

Financial inclusion data

There are two main data sources on financial inclusion covering a large set of European countries: the Global Findex collected by Gallup and the World Bank in 2011 and 2014 (Demirguc-Kunt et al. 2012, 2015) and several waves of the Eurobarometer collected in 2003, 2005 (Special Eurobarometer 230 / Wave 63.2), and 2011 (Special Eurobarometer 373, wave 76.1).

The Global Findex covers the adult population aged 15+ in 39 European countries. It provides data on the percentage of respondents with an account (individually or jointly with someone else) at a bank, credit union, other financial institution (e.g., cooperative, microfinance institution).

Eurobarometer covers the population of European Union Member States (27 countries) aged 15 years and over.

Table D.1 provides a comparison of data on bank account holding between the Global Findex and Eurobarometer. Percentages are similar for most countries, with the exceptions on Lithuania (where Eurobarometer reports a higher level of financial inclusion than the Global Findex by about 11 percentage points) and Bulgaria, Ireland, Malta and Romania (where the Global Findex reports a higher level of financial inclusion than Eurobarometer by over 10 percentage points).

As Eurobarometer collected similar data in different years, it allows researchers and policy makers to get some insights on the improvement in financial inclusion over time. Table D.2 shows the percentage of the population aged 15+ who held a current account and/or a deposit account in 2005 and the percentage of adults of the same age who held a bank account in 2011. Bank account holding appears to have increased in every country, with the exception of Malta (but results should be interpreted with caution due to the changing definition over time).

Finally, Eurobarometer also provides data on the percentage of respondents who held various financial products in 2011, including bank accounts, mortgages, credit cards, personal loans, shares or bonds, investment funds, life insurance and other types of insurance (see Table D.3).

Table D.1. **Bank account holding**

Percentage of the population aged 15+ holding a specific product

	Account at a financial institution (Findex)		Bank account (Eurobarometer)
	2014	**2011**	**2011**
Albania	37.99	28.27	--
Armenia	17.24	17.49	--
Austria	96.73	97.08	92.05
Azerbaijan	29.15	14.90	--
Belarus	71.98	58.60	--
Belgium	98.13	96.31	94.85
Bosnia and Herzegovina	52.69	56.21	--
Bulgaria	62.99	52.82	27.71
Croatia	86.03	88.39	--
Czech Republic	82.18	80.65	82.26
Denmark	100.00	99.74	99.53
Estonia	97.67	96.82	93.74
Finland	100.00	99.65	99.05
France	96.58	96.98	96.09
FYROM	71.80	73.70	
Georgia	39.67	32.98	--
Germany	98.76	98.13	95.47
Greece	87.52	77.94	80.08
Hungary	72.26	72.67	67.48
Ireland	94.71	93.89	82.03
Italy	87.33	71.01	74.83
Latvia	90.22	89.66	83.76
Lithuania	77.91	73.76	82.98
Luxembourg	96.17	94.59	96.93
Malta	96.33	95.27	70.24
Moldova	17.76	18.07	--
Montenegro	59.83	50.44	--
Netherlands	99.30	98.66	98.87
Poland	77.86	70.19	67.51
Portugal	87.39	81.23	80.01
Romania	60.79	48.18	26.98
Russian Federation	67.38	44.59	--
Serbia	83.09	62.22	--
Slovak Republic	77.24	79.58	77.25
Slovenia	97.24	97.14	95.60
Spain	97.58	93.28	88.45
Sweden	99.72	98.99	98.29
Turkey	56.51	57.60	--
Ukraine	52.71	41.27	--
United Kingdom	98.93	97.20	91.53

Sources: Demirguc-Kunt et al. (2012, 2015) and Eurobarometer (2012)

Table D.2. **Bank account holding, 2005-2011**

Percentage of the population aged 15+ holding a specific product

	Current account 2005	Deposit account 2005	Current account and/or deposit account 2005	Bank account 2011
Austria	73.06	56.47	84.10	92.05
Belgium	92.51	68.37	94.78	94.85
Czech Republic	73.45	14.12	78.82	82.26
Denmark	47.17	26.15	61.88	99.53
Estonia	73.51	14.55	77.93	93.74
Finland	82.37	30.78	87.26	99.05
France	86.58	20.55	89.36	96.09
Germany	91.33	39.45	94.34	95.47
Greece	9.60	59.05	65.24	80.08
Hungary	49.49	8.94	54.05	67.48
Ireland	56.64	36.36	72.32	82.03
Italy	62.33	8.81	69.83	74.83
Latvia	28.56	6.56	32.22	83.76
Lithuania	41.53	8.75	46.72	82.98
Luxembourg	73.58	29.37	84.96	96.93
Malta	52.68	46.46	75.21	70.24
Netherlands	95.34	30.15	95.70	98.87
Poland	46.03	7.89	49.29	67.51
Portugal	73.62	12.49	76.99	80.01
Slovakia	62.07	20.09	73.55	77.25
Slovenia	87.09	7.77	89.74	95.60
Spain	50.04	54.00	88.72	88.45
Sweden	74.86	50.12	84.66	98.29
United Kingdom	75.06	36.09	82.00	91.53

Source: Eurobarometer (2005, 2012)

Table D.3. **Financial products holding, 2011**

Percentage of the population aged 15+ holding a specific product

	Bank account	Mortgage	Credit card	Personal loan	Shares or bonds	Investment fund	Life insurance	Other insurance
Austria	92.05	5.56	30.07	18.15	8.83	7.44	41.27	65.66
Belgium	94.85	26.36	53.62	13.75	15.62	7.21	38.95	66.87
Bulgaria	27.71	2.47	11.91	15.1	0.15	0.22	5.12	20.08
Czech Republic	82.26	9.25	25.12	15.42	1.81	2.48	36.33	61.77
Denmark	99.53	48.17	70.51	32.02	43.6	14.41	52.55	86.43
Estonia	93.74	11.64	31.16	15.78	2.92	5.94	15.36	37.71
Finland	99.05	31.91	59.79	21.42	24.68	8.94	38.11	78.73
France	96.09	22.39	74.46	17.64	16.36	2.94	44.83	60.89
Germany	95.47	10.64	34.02	8.84	12.2	10.56	34.03	53.91
Greece	80.08	10.94	18.14	13.24	2.8	0.61	6.25	34.08
Hungary	67.48	13.47	8.7	11.4	1.66	0.76	19.01	30.18
Ireland	82.03	29.77	44.56	25.41	11.55	8.39	37.49	69.91
Italy	74.83	14.57	31.34	9.32	6.24	7.45	15.48	43.46
Latvia	83.76	7.54	40.68	6.94	2.18	1.69	14.82	31.86
Lithuania	82.98	1.41	16.31	9.82	2.31	1.63	14.24	34.73
Luxembourg	96.93	35.38	87.17	17.94	18.49	9.97	43.16	72.96
Malta	70.24	16.55	58.64	8.51	21.26	16.16	27.44	59.74
Netherlands	98.87	52.87	51.99	8.48	23.42	3.56	40.95	88.4
Poland	67.51	5.78	19.18	11.64	3.06	2.64	32.51	25.48
Portugal	80.01	18.86	18.79	6.47	2.21	1.82	18.97	31.81
Romania	26.98	3.39	16.88	12.5	0.78	0.38	8.25	33.82
Slovakia	77.25	10.53	23.91	13.93	2.77	2.77	41.93	66.47
Slovenia	95.6	3.91	42.86	15.48	13.95	10.4	49.49	83.11
Spain	88.45	26.26	46.04	15.04	4.02	5.46	22.02	52.12
Sweden	98.29	44.9	58.94	28.92	45.73	29.99	60.41	87.95
United Kingdom	91.53	26.85	47.89	13.6	20.82	12.74	37.17	51.15

Source: Eurobarometer (2012)

Annex E

Financial knowledge questions in the 2015 OECD/INFE Toolkit for Measuring Financial Literacy and Financial Inclusion

Table E.1. **Text of the financial knowledge questions (2015 OECD/INFE Toolkit for Measuring Financial Literacy and Financial Inclusion**
($=national currency)

Standard question – 2015 OECD/INFE Toolkit for Measuring Financial Literacy and Financial Inclusion	**Purpose**
Imagine that five brothers are given a gift of $1000 in total. If the brothers have to share the money equally how much does each one get? [Open response: $200]	To test ability to undertake basic mental arithmetic in a financial context.
Now imagine that the brothers have to wait for one year to get their share of the $1000 and inflation stays at X percent. In one year's time will they be able to buy. a) More with their share of the money than they could today; b) The same amount; c) Or, less than they could buy today. d) It depends on the types of things that they want to buy; e) Don't know	To test ability to understand how inflation impacts on purchasing power.
You lend $25 to a friend one evening and he gives you $25 back the next day. How much interest has he paid on this loan? [Open response: 0]	To test understanding of interest without difficult arithmetic.
Suppose you put $100 into a <no fee, tax free> savings account with a guaranteed interest rate of 2% per year. You don't make any further payments into this account and you don't withdraw any money. How much would be in the account at the end of the first year, once the interest payment is made? [Open response: $102]	To test ability to calculate simple interest on savings.

Table E.1. **Text of the financial knowledge questions (2015 OECD/INFE Toolkit for Measuring Financial Literacy and Financial Inclusion** (cont.).
($=national currency)

Standard question –	**Purpose**
..and how much would be in the account at the end of five years [add if necessary: remembering there are no fees or tax deductions]? Would it be... a) More than $110 b) Exactly $110 c) Less than $110 d) Or is it impossible to tell from the information given	To test whether respondent is aware of the additional benefit of compounding.
An investment with a high return is likely to be high risk/ or *if someone offers you the chance to make a lot of money it is likely that there is also a chance that you will lose a lot of money.* [True/False]	To test whether respondent understands the typical relationship between risk and return.
High inflation means that the cost of living is increasing rapidly [True/False]	To test understanding of the meaning of the term inflation.
It is usually possible to reduce the risk of investing in the stock market by buying a wide range of stocks and shares or *it is less likely that you will lose all of your money if you save it in more than one place.* [True/False]	To test whether respondent is aware of the benefit of diversification.

ORGANISATION FOR ECONOMIC CO-OPERATION AND DEVELOPMENT

The OECD is a unique forum where governments work together to address the economic, social and environmental challenges of globalisation. The OECD is also at the forefront of efforts to understand and to help governments respond to new developments and concerns, such as corporate governance, the information economy and the challenges of an ageing population. The Organisation provides a setting where governments can compare policy experiences, seek answers to common problems, identify good practice and work to co-ordinate domestic and international policies.

The OECD member countries are: Australia, Austria, Belgium, Canada, Chile, the Czech Republic, Denmark, Estonia, Finland, France, Germany, Greece, Hungary, Iceland, Ireland, Israel, Italy, Japan, Korea, Luxembourg, Mexico, the Netherlands, New Zealand, Norway, Poland, Portugal, the Slovak Republic, Slovenia, Spain, Sweden, Switzerland, Turkey, the United Kingdom and the United States. The European Union takes part in the work of the OECD.

OECD Publishing disseminates widely the results of the Organisation's statistics gathering and research on economic, social and environmental issues, as well as the conventions, guidelines and standards agreed by its members.

OECD PUBLISHING, 2, rue André-Pascal, 75775 PARIS CEDEX 16
(21 2016 01 1 P) ISBN 978-92-64-25424-4 – 2016

www.ingramcontent.com/pod-product-compliance
Lightning Source LLC
LaVergne TN
LVHW081422110826
845149LV00010B/1835

* 9 7 8 9 2 6 4 2 5 4 2 4 4 *